Wonderful World

By Amy Bauman and Jim Pipe

tick tock

North American edition copyright © **ticktock Entertainment Ltd.** 2010

First published in North America in 2010 by **ticktock Media Ltd**.
The Old Sawmill, Goods Station Road, Tunbridge Wells, Kent TN1 2DP, U.K.

ticktock project editor: Ruth Owen
ticktock picture researcher: Ruth Owen
Project designer: Emma Randall
With thanks to: Suzy Gazlay, Terry Jennings, Jean Coppendale, Elaine Wilkinson, Vicky Crichton, Emma Dods, and Claire Lucas

ISBN 978-1-84696-204-2
Tracking Number: 3232LPP1009

Printed in China
9 8 7 6 5 4 3 2 1

All rights reserved. No part of this publication may be reproduced, copied, stored in a retrieval system, or transmitted in any form or by any means electronic, mechanical, photocopying, recording, or otherwise without prior written permission of the copyright owner.

Picture credits (t=top; b=bottom; c=center; l=left; r=right; OFC=outside front cover;
OBC=outside back cover; A–Z=from top to bottom):
age fotostock/SuperStock: 14–15, 32–33, 76b, 77tr, 77cr, 91br, 97tl, 98b. Arctic-Images/Corbis: 104b. Manfred Bail/Image Broker/FLPA: 100tl, 110l E. Jim Brandenburg/Minden Pictures/FLPA: 71bl. Bridgeman Art Library, London/SuperStock: 29r F. Mark Cassino/SuperStock: 32cl, 49tl. Nigel Cattlin/FLPA: 69br. Bruce Coleman: 83cr. Corbis: 22–23. Corbis/SuperStock: 23cr. Creatas/SuperStock: 50cl. Christian Darkin/Science Photo Library: 18c. Marcos Delgado/epa/Corbis: 52–53. Digital Stock: 61cbr. Digital Vision Ltd./SuperStock: 84t, 85bl. Gerry Ellis/Minden Pictures/FLPA: 59. Eye of Science/Science Photo Library: 29c. Chris Fallows: 66t. Michael & Patricia Fogden/Minden Pictures/FLPA: 72tl. Dean Fox/SuperStock: 96. Getty Images: 109 main. David T. Grewcock/FLPA: 100cl. David Halbakken/Alamy: 47tr. John Henshall/Alamy: 32bl. Steele Hill/NASA/Science Photo Library: 17b. Michio Hoshino/Minden Pictures/FLPA: 63. Ingram Publishing/SuperStock: 72 main, 94–95. iStock: 29r D, 56–57, 99, 109tr. Jupiter Images/Comstock Images/Alamy: 51br. A. Simon-Miller/GSFC/NASA/ESA/STScI/Science Photo Library: 50bl. NASA: 6 all, 6–7 main, 9br, 32tl, 74tl, 83br. North Wind Picture Archives/Alamy: 33br. Photodisc: 85tl, 85tr. Photodisc/SuperStock: 86l. Pixtal/SuperStock: 37t. Fritz Polking/FLPA: 77br. Powerstock/SuperStock: 81br. Reuters/Mariana Bazo: 24c. Michel Roggo/naturepl.com: 62b. Shutterstock: OFC all, 1 all, 3, 4–5, 7tr, 7cr, 7br, 8t, 8b, 9tr, 9cr, 10–11, 11c, 11tr, 11cr, 11br, 12cl, 12cl, 12–13, 13t, 16t, 16b, 16–17, 17tr, 18t, 22t, 23tr, 25 main, 26fl, 26tl, 26cl, 26bl, 26–27, 27tr, 27cr, 28b, 29r A, B, C, E, 30–31, 32fl, 32cl, 32–33, 33tr, 33cr, 34–35, 35tr, 35bl, 35br, 36t, 37b, 38 main, 38b, 39bl, 39br, 40cl, 40bl, 40–41, 42tl, 42cl, 42bl, 43t, 44 all, 45 all, 46l x3, 46c, 46–47, 48cl, 48bl, 48–49, 49tr, 50tl, 52tl, 52bl, 53tr, 53bl, 54–55, 56fl, 56 x3, 57 x3, 58 all, 61tl, 61cl, 61cr, 61bl, 61br, 62t, 64 all, 65t, 68–69, 68 all, 69bl, 69bc, 70, 71c, 71tr, 71cr, 74–75, 78–79, 80fl, 80tl, 80cl, 80bl, 80–81, 81tr, 81cr, 83tl, 83bl, 84b, 85cl, 85cr, 85br, 86–87, 88l, 88–89b, 91tr, 92l, 92br, 93tr, 93cr, 93br, 93b x3, 95r x3, 97tr, 97br, 98t, 100–101, 101t, 102–103, 104–105, 105br, 106 all, 107 all, 108 all, 110l A, B, C, D, F, 111r A, B, C, D, E, G, OBC all. Jurgen & Christine Sohns/FLPA: 60, 71br. Stock Image/SuperStock: 42 main. SuperStock Inc./SuperStock: 8–9, 26b, 27br. Soqui Ted/Corbis Sygma: 89t. The Natural History Museum, London: 19t. ThinkStock/SuperStock: 90–91. ticktock Media Archive: 10t, 10b, 12bl, 15b, 18b, 19b, 20t, 20b, 21, 22b, 23br, 24tl, 24cl, 24bl, 25 x4, 28t, 33t, 35t, 36b, 38tr, 39tr, 40tl, 41tr, 41c, 43b, bl, 50–51, 51t, 65b, 66b, 67 all, 73, 80b, 83tr, 87c, 87r all, 88t, 90bl, 90br, 100bl, 104tl, 105cr (t and b), 110t, 110l G, 111r F. Quilla Ulmer/im Reed Photography Science Photo Library: 48tl. Steve Vilder/SuperStock: 75cr, 82. Tony Waltham/Robert Harding World Imagery/Corbis: 92–93t. Konrad Wothe/Minden Pictures/FLPA: 76–77. Norbert Wu/Minden Pictures/FLPA: 75tr.

Every effort has been made to trace copyright holders, and we apologize in advance for any omissions.
We would be pleased to insert the appropriate acknowledgments in any subsequent edition of this publication.

CONTENTS

Part One: The Making of Planet Earth

Chapter 1: Our Amazing Planet   6
Chapter 2: Earth's Layers   12
Chapter 3: Our Restless Earth   18
Chapter 4: Changing Face of Earth   22
Chapter 5: Earth's Building Materials   26

Part Two: Earth's Weather and Climate

Chapter 6: The World's Weather   32
Chapter 7: Everyday Weather   40
Chapter 8: Extreme Weather   50

Part Three: Earth's Ecosystems

Chapter 9: What Is an Ecosystem?   56
Chapter 10: How Ecosystems Work   60
Chapter 11: Living in an Ecosystem   66
Chapter 12: Biomes   72

Part Four: Earth's Natural Resources

Chapter 13: What Are Natural Resources?   80
Chapter 14: Nonrenewable Resources   86
Chapter 15: Renewable Resources   94

Part Five: Caring for Planet Earth

Chapter 16: Climate Change   104
Chapter 17: Making a Difference   106

Glossary   110
Index   112

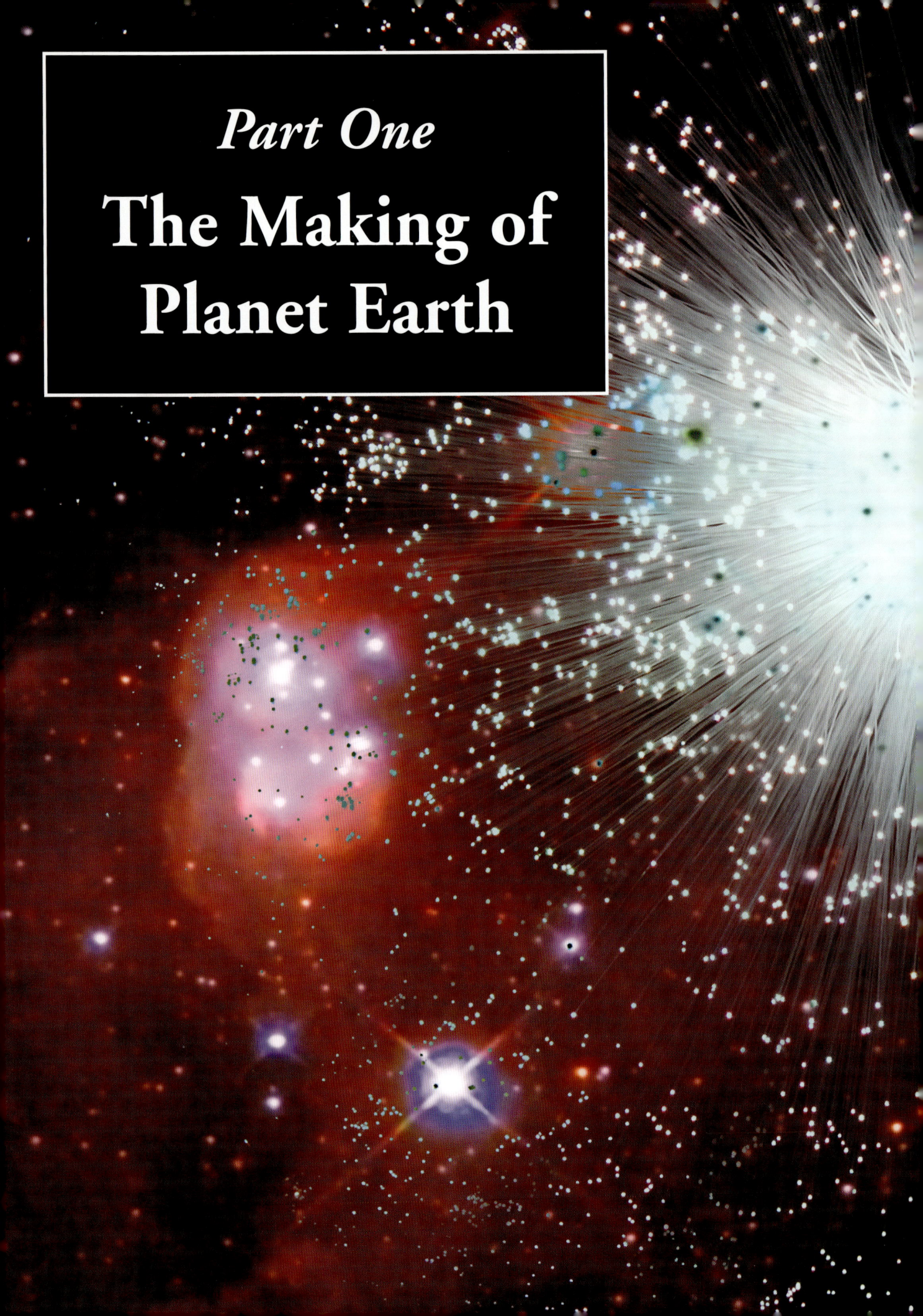

Part One
The Making of Planet Earth

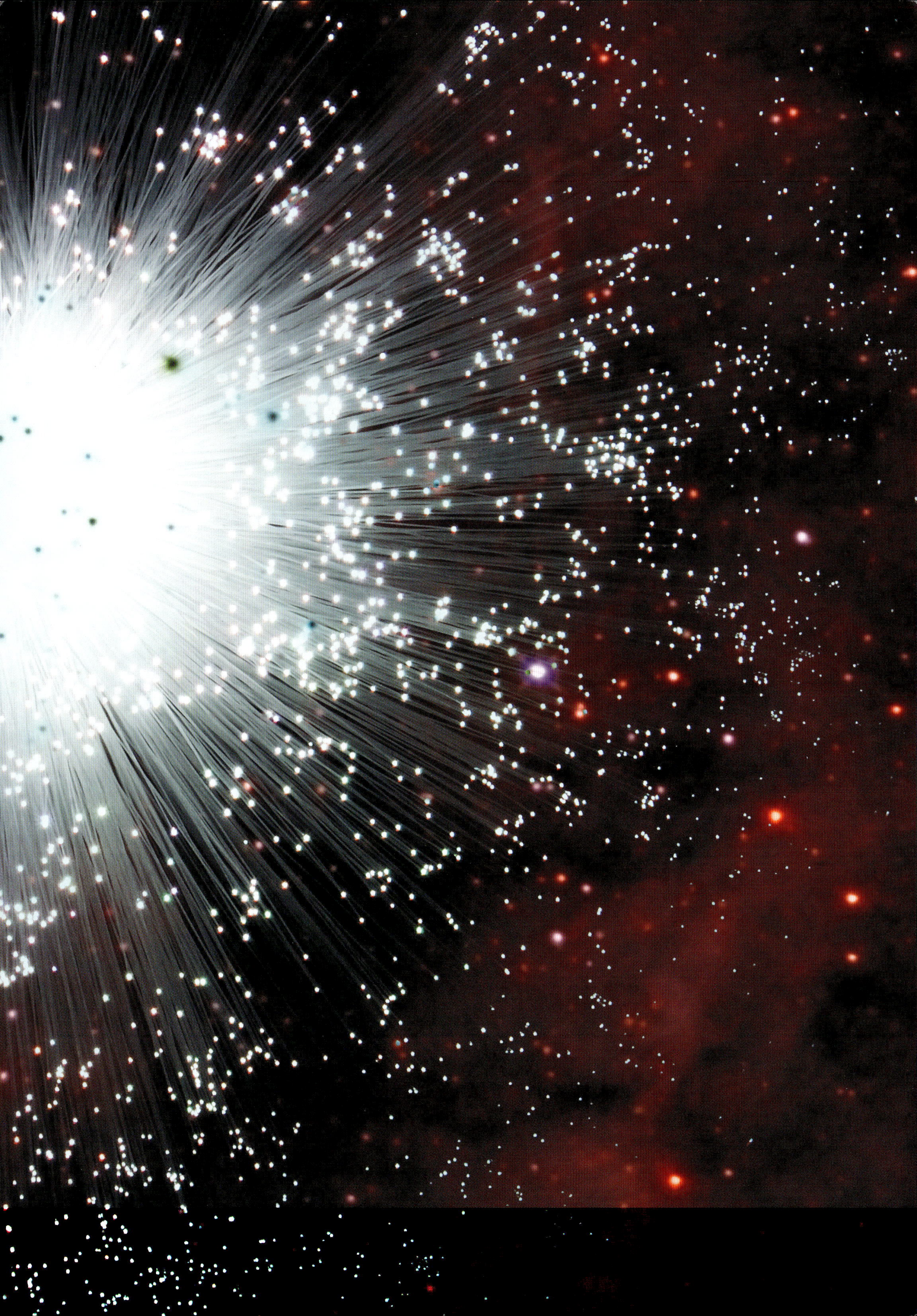

WONDERFUL WORLD

The Moon is located 238,300 mi. (384,400km) from Earth.

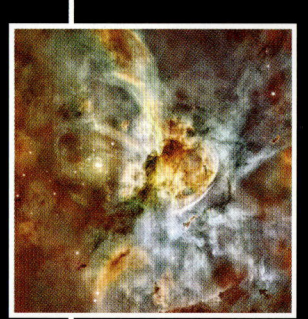

From a cloud of gas and dust . . .

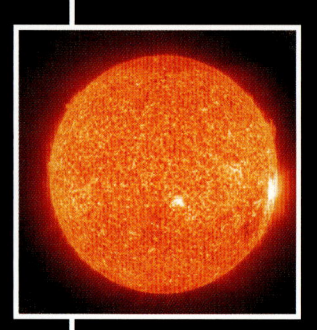

. . . our Sun was born. Rocks, metal, and dust left over from the Sun's creation formed big rocky clumps . . .

. . . that became the planets of our solar system.

CHAPTER 1: Our Amazing Planet

Our Earth is a ball of rock hurtling through space at around 67,000 mph (108,000km/h). Using satellites we can see the surface of Earth from space. We can see that its rocky surface is covered in vast blue stretches of water. Green plant life springs from the soil. And if we move closer, we can see towering rocky mountains and deep valleys.

BIRTH OF THE PLANET

Our planet's history began more than 4.5 billion years ago. Scientists believe that at that time, our solar system was a huge cloud of dust and gas floating in space. Then the cloud began to collapse. The dust and gas spiraled inward.

Out of the dust and gas came a newly formed star—our Sun. Some of the dust particles that were left spinning around the Sun began to join together. They formed large chunks of rocks. Some of these rocks were small enough to fit in your hand. Others were as large as mountains. These rocky chunks joined together and grew until they became rocky planets. One of these planets became Earth.

OUR AMAZING PLANET

Planet Earth is around 93 million mi. (150 million km) from the Sun—the third planet from the Sun in our solar system. This "just right" position—neither too close nor too far—keeps the temperature of our planet moderate and stable. This is one factor that makes life possible on Earth.

White clouds float in the atmosphere (the layer of gases that covers our planet).

PLANET EARTH FACTS

EARTH'S INGREDIENTS
Planet Earth is made up mostly of only eight elements. These are aluminum, calcium, iron, magnesium, oxygen, potassium, silicon, and sodium. Silicon and oxygen make up around 75 percent of Earth's rocks.

THE BLUE PLANET
Earth is a unique planet in our solar system. It is the only planet that has large quantities of liquid water on its surface. Without this water, there would be no life on Earth.

AN EARTH YEAR
It takes Earth 365 days, six hours, nine minutes, and ten seconds to orbit the Sun. To complete one orbit, Earth travels 583,709,069 mi. (941,466,240km).

BIRTH OF THE MOON
The Moon is Earth's only natural satellite. Scientists believe the Moon formed not too long after Earth was created. One of the huge whirling masses of rock that were circling the Sun collided with Earth. Debris from the collision exploded into space and began circling Earth. There the debris formed the Moon in the same way that Earth was formed.

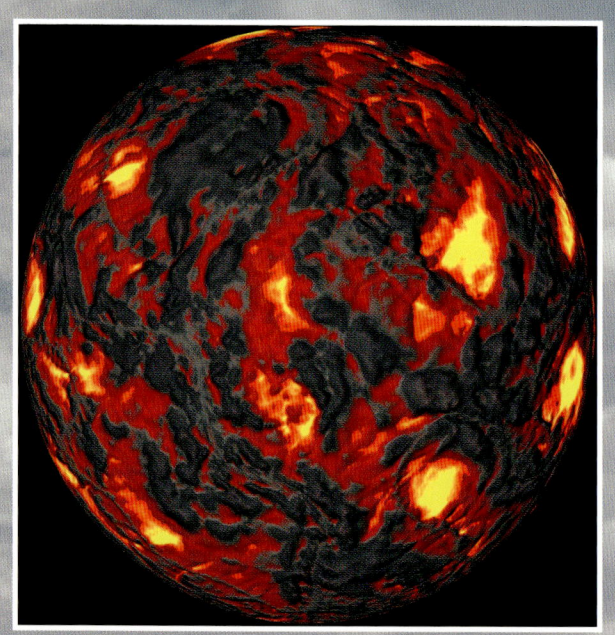

EARTH'S EARLY YEARS

As debris from space continued to pound young Earth, the planet's surface heated and melted. Eventually, scientists believe, it became a huge sea of molten rock and metal. Each new particle of matter added to the mix and increased the planet's size.

At the same time, the molten rock released nitrogen, carbon dioxide, and water vapor into the air. To this, the stream of debris added a lot of of dust. An atmosphere began forming around the planet, but it was a dark, dusty, and poisonous one!

Scientists are not sure when Earth's surface began to form a crust. But rocks around 3.8 billion years old have been found in Canada. Around this time, Earth's surface began to become solid.

This illustration shows Earth as it might have looked during its molten phase. As our planet was forming, so were other planets. Eventually, around 4.3 billion years ago, our entire solar system took shape—eight planets orbiting the Sun.

EXTINCTION LEVEL EVENT

The Chicxulub crater in Mexico has an impact crater of around 105 mi. (170km) in diameter. Scientists believe the impact was caused by an asteroid or meteorite with a diameter of around 6 mi. (10km). The impact happened around 65 million years ago. It would have led to earthquakes, firestorms, tsunamis, and catastrophic devastation on Earth's surface. Some scientists believe this collision with space debris caused the dinosaurs to beome extinct.

METEORITES

Today, pieces of rock and metal are still shooting through space. Most of these bits of space debris burn up when they hit Earth's atmosphere. But sometimes they make it to the surface. When they do, we call them meteorites.

EVIDENCE OF PAST COLLISIONS

Earth's crust is marked by craters from prehistoric collisions between the planet and meteorites. Scientists estimate that over the past one billion years there have been around 130,000 impacts that have produced craters with a diameter of 0.60 mi. (1km) or larger.

Meteor crater in Arizona was formed between 20,000 and 50,000 years ago. The crater measures 0.70 mi. (1.2m) in diameter. It was made by an asteroid measuring around 79 ft. (24m) in diameter and was the first crater on Earth to be identified as an impact crater.

SPACE DEBRIS

Leftover debris from the formation of our solar system is identified in the following ways:

METEORS/METEORITES
Meteors are chunks of rock and metal. As they enter Earth's atmosphere, they burn up and make a streak of light. When they do this, we call them shooting stars. A meteor that hits Earth is known as a meteorite.

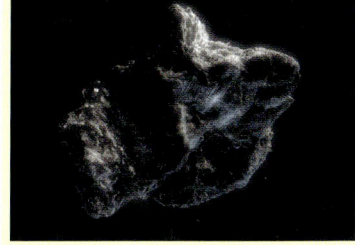

ASTEROIDS
Asteroids are jagged, rocky bodies. Most are found orbiting the Sun between Mars and Jupiter in an area called the asteroid belt. Some asteroids can be almost 620 mi. (1,000km) across.

COMETS
Comets are balls of frozen gas, dust, and rock that orbit the Sun. As a comet gets close to the Sun, some of the ice on its surface evaporates. This releases dust, forming a tail. A comet's dust tail can be 6.2 million mi. (10 million km) long.

PLANET EARTH: INSIDE AND OUT

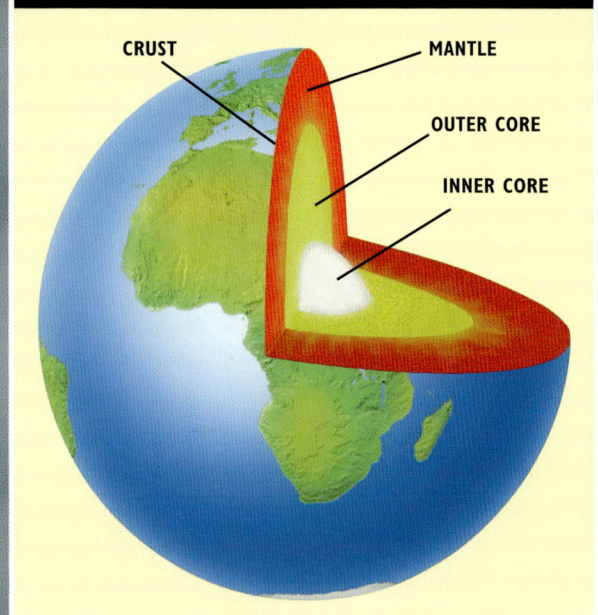

- CRUST
- MANTLE
- OUTER CORE
- INNER CORE

DIAMETER AT THE EQUATOR:
7,909 mi. (12,756km)

DIAMETER AT THE POLES:
7,883 mi. (12,714km)

CIRCUMFERENCE AT THE EQUATOR:
24,847 mi. (40,075km)

WEIGHT (MASS) OF EARTH:
6.6 sextillion tons

DISTANCE FROM THE SUN:
93,000,000 mi. (150,000,000km)

AVERAGE SURFACE TEMPERATURE:
59°F (15°C)

THE PLANET AS WE KNOW IT

Earth's surface began to cool and form a crust. But even then, the planet was molten inside. Melted rock, called magma, churned and flowed and sometimes still burst onto the planet's surface.

All this heat and movement released huge amounts of water vapor into the young planet's atmosphere. More water was brought to the planet by comets.

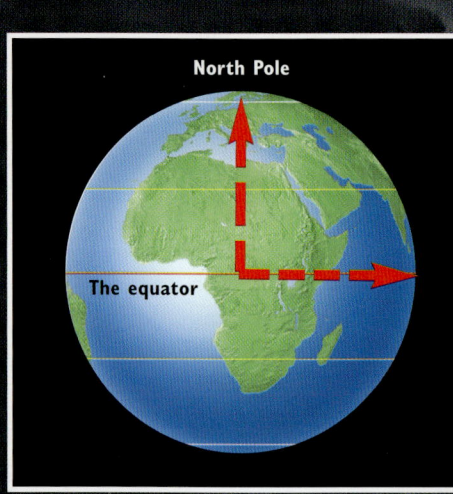

RADIUS OF THE SPHERE

Earth is not a perfect sphere. If it were, its radius at the poles would be the same as its radius at the equator. Earth has a slight bulge at the equator. Therefore, at this location, the planet's radius is slightly greater than at the poles. There is a difference of around 26 mi. (42km) between the two measurements.

All this water together was then taken up into the atmosphere. There the water gathered, only to rain back down onto the planet. Low spots on Earth's surface filled with water, and oceans, lakes, and rivers developed. Earth, as we know it, began to take shape.

Today, our active planet is still cooling. But between its birth and the present day, Earth's structure has divided into three distinct layers. We call the three layers the crust, the mantle, and the core.

Mount Chimborazo in Ecuador sits on the equator. The diameter of Earth is greater at the equator than at the poles. So the top of Mount Chimborazo is actually the farthest point from the center of Earth!

Kilauea volcano, on Hawaii Island, pours molten lava into the ocean.

MAGMA AND LAVA

SHAPING FROM WITHIN
Here, magma can be seen beneath Earth's crust. Lava is magma that has reached Earth's surface. When lava pours from beneath Earth's crust, it shapes the surface. This is one of the ways that scientists believe the planet developed.

ADDING TO THE LANDSCAPE
New lava flows out of and over previous flows. Just as with Earth's early crust, the lava cools and hardens at uneven speeds.

NEW TERRAIN
These plants are growing on a hillside formed from cooled lava and volcanic ash. After a volcano erupts, water, wind, heat, and cold break down the rocks and carry in sand and debris. Patches of soil form where seeds can grow.

WONDERFUL WORLD

HIGHS AND LOWS

MOUNT EVEREST
Mount Everest is a peak in the Himalaya Mountains. It is the highest point on Earth. Mount Everest is located between Nepal and Tibet. It stands 29,000 ft. (8,850m) tall.

THE DEAD SEA
The lowest point on Earth not covered by water or ice is along the shore of the Dead Sea. This salty inland sea borders Israel and Jordan. The shore is 1,300 ft. (400m) below sea level.

CHALLENGER DEEP
If we include places on Earth's crust that are under the ocean, the Challenger Deep is the lowest point below sea level. This section of the Marianas Trench is in the northwest Pacific Ocean. Challenger Deep is 35,831 ft. (10,924m) deep.

CHAPTER 2:
Earth's Layers

Earth's crust is the most visible part of the planet and the part we know best. The soaring mountains, deep valleys, and seemingly bottomless ocean trenches make Earth's crust seem "rock solid" and almost indestructible. In reality, the crust is the thinnest and most fragile of Earth's layers. If you think of Earth as an apple, the crust is like the apple's skin!

EARTH'S LAYERS

EARTH'S BRITTLE CRUST

Earth's landscape differs from place to place. This means the thickness of the crust is also different. It is thicker where there are high mountains and thinner in deep trenches. Beneath the oceans, the crust is generally around 4 mi. (7km) thick. Where there are landmasses, the crust has an average depth of around 25 mi. (40km). Because the planet is covered by so much water, 70 percent of Earth's crust is under oceans.

Uluru is a rocky outcrop in Uluru-Kata Tjuta National Park in central Australia. It stands 1,141 ft. (348m) high. Scientists believe Uluru is the remains of an earlier mountain range. You can see the different layers of Earth's crust in the stripes on its side.

The Grand Canyon in Arizona allows us to see deep into Earth's layered crust. The canyon is 277 mi. (446km) long and around 6,000 ft. (1,829m) deep at its lowest point.

THE MANTLE
The mantle is the layer beneath the crust. It is the thickest of Earth's layers, with an average depth of 1,800 mi. (2,900km). It is thought to be made mostly of silicon and oxygen.

UPPER MANTLE
The uppermost layer of the mantle is rigid like Earth's crust. Below this is the thin asthenosphere layer. At this sublayer, it starts to get very hot. Temperatures may reach 1,600ºF (870ºC)—hot enough to make you melt!

Scientists believe that the asthenosphere is generally semisolid. But, under heat and pressure, it can become soft enough to flow—slowly. Then it may be more like melted tar.

HOT SPOTS
A hot spot is an especially hot upper-mantle area. Hot spots form when magma from Earth's mantle rises to the surface. People in Iceland enjoy the benefits of living on a hot spot. Boiling magma close to the surface naturally heats lakes and pools. People can swim outside even during the winter!

This is the Blue Lagoon in Iceland, which is a pool whose water comes from the runoff of the nearby Svartsengi power plant. There, steam from the natural hot water is used to drive turbines to produce environmentally friendly electricity. Swimmers enjoy the naturally warm water, too.

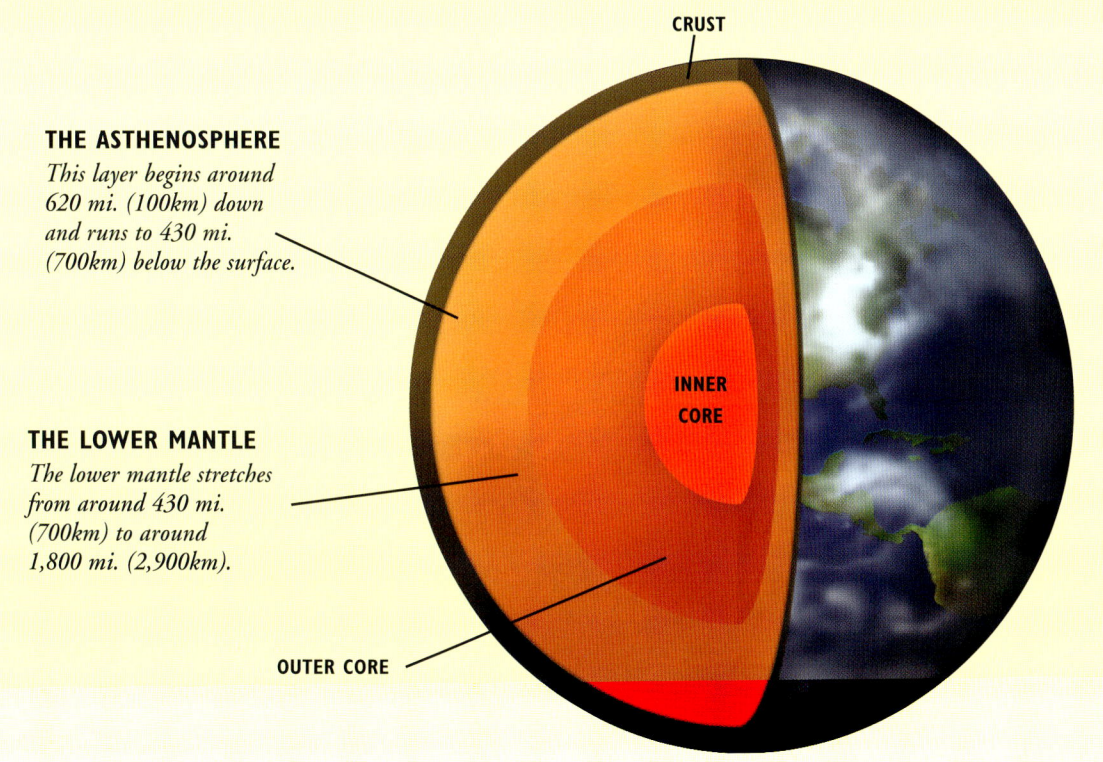

EARTH'S LAYERS

LOWER MANTLE

The lower mantle is made mostly of silicate rocks (rocks composed of silica, oxygen, and metals). There is also a lot of iron and magnesium. Moving toward the core, both pressure and heat increase. At the edge of the core, temperatures may reach 4,000ºF (2,200ºC).

EARTH'S MANTLE

THE ASTHENOSPHERE
This layer begins around 620 mi. (100km) down and runs to 430 mi. (700km) below the surface.

THE LOWER MANTLE
The lower mantle stretches from around 430 mi. (700km) to around 1,800 mi. (2,900km).

CRUST

INNER CORE

OUTER CORE

JOURNEY TO THE CENTER OF EARTH

Scientists believe that at Earth's outer core the average temperature is around 7,200–9,000°F (4,000–5,000°C).

In the inner core, temperatures may be as high as 9,000–12,600°F (5,000–7,000°C). It is probably as hot as the surface of the Sun.

EARTH'S CORE

Earth's core is the layer that scientists know the least about. They believe it is made up of two mini layers—an outer molten liquid layer and a solid inner layer.

Earth's outer core is made mostly of molten iron and nickel. It is around 1,400 mi. (2,300km) thick.

Earth's inner core is also thought to be made of metals such as iron and nickel. Because the materials are under great pressure at this depth, the core stays solid.

A blacksmith heats metal to make a horseshoe. The red-hot metal looks like lava and becomes soft. It behaves just like the metals of Earth's outer core.

EARTH'S LAYERS

EARTH'S CORE AND ITS MAGNETIC FIELD

Earth's outer core is molten metal. As this mass moves, it spins the solid inner core of the planet. Scientists believe this motion, along with the core's heat, produces an electric current. The current creates a magnetic field around the planet, so Earth behaves like a giant magnet.

The magnetic field that surrounds Earth is called the magnetosphere. It is a powerful force that makes a compass point north.

This is a meteorite from Canyon Diablo in Arizona. The meteorite is made of iron and nickel—the same ingredients as Earth's core.

The compass is an old tool. It was invented in China. Compasses were used by sailors and travelers to check in which direction they were moving.

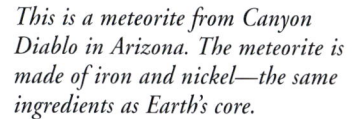

OUR PROTECTIVE SHIELD

The magnetosphere, Earth's magnetic field, has several important roles. Among them is to act as a protective layer for the planet. This layer keeps out harmful materials from space, including solar wind. Solar wind is a flow of particles from the Sun. Like magnets, these particles have a charge. If they reached Earth, they could be destructive. Thanks to the magnetosphere, that does not happen often. This illustration shows the magnetosphere (blue) forcing the particles (orange) out and around the planet.

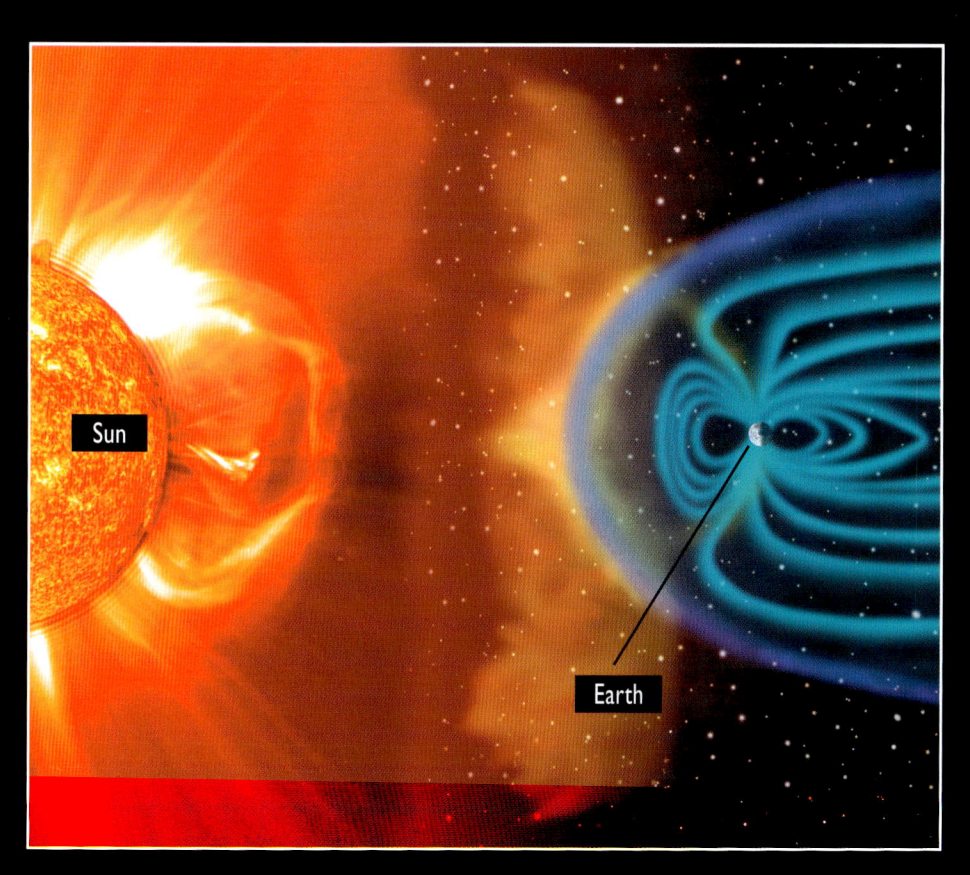

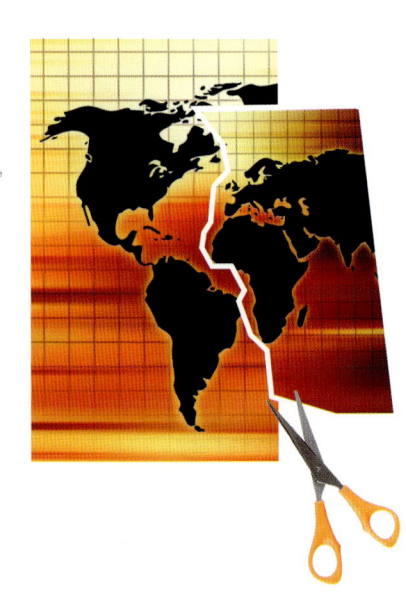

CHAPTER 3:
Our Restless Earth

Look at a map of the world. Do you think it's possible that if there were no oceans between the continents, the landmasses might fit together? For example, would the west of Africa fit around the north of South America?

PANGAEA

In the late 1800s and early 1900s, scientists began to study this idea. They investigated the theory that Earth's continents were once a single huge piece of land. In 1912, German scientist Alfred Wegener (1880–1930) named this giant landmass Pangaea.

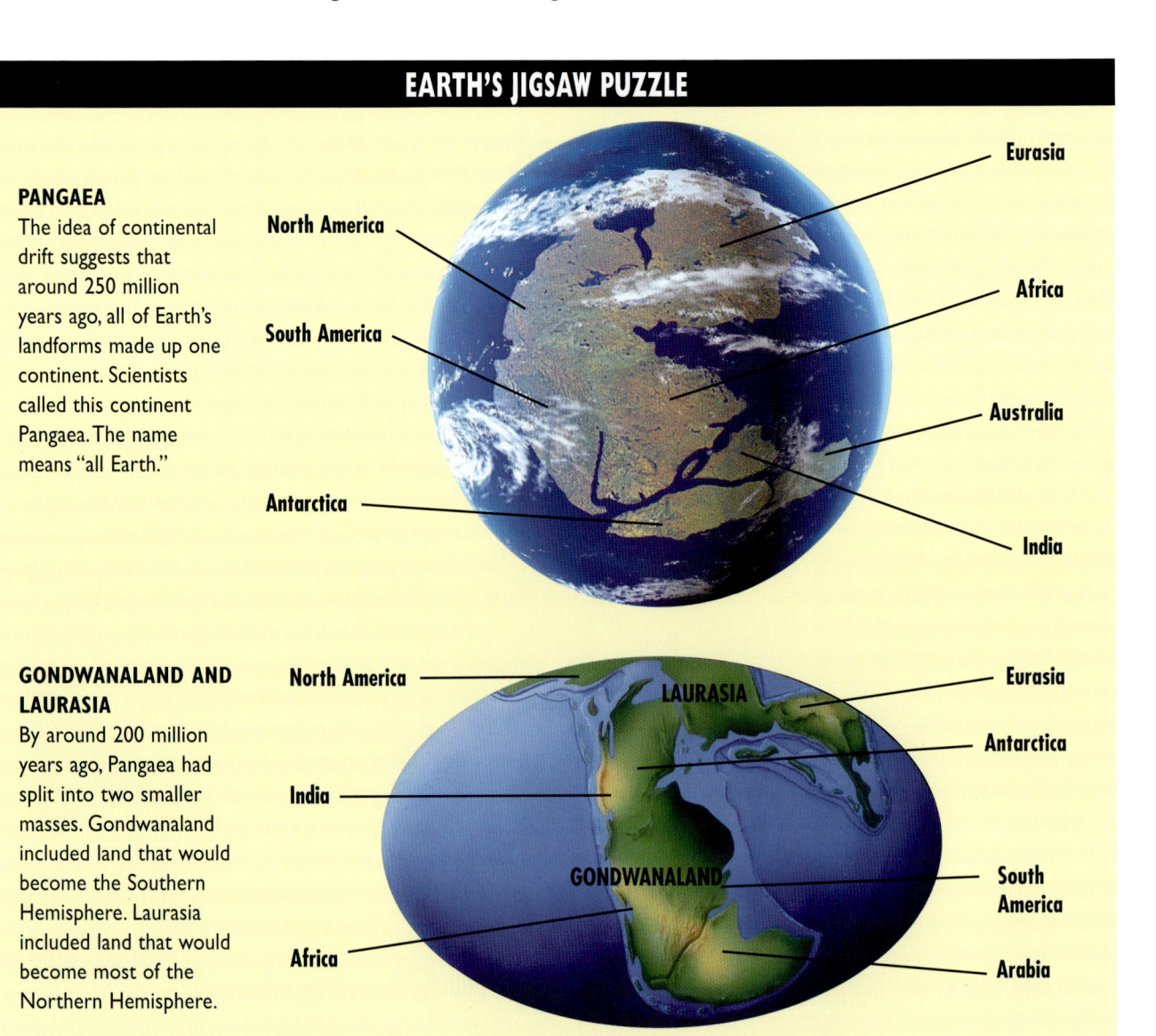

EARTH'S JIGSAW PUZZLE

PANGAEA
The idea of continental drift suggests that around 250 million years ago, all of Earth's landforms made up one continent. Scientists called this continent Pangaea. The name means "all Earth."

GONDWANALAND AND LAURASIA
By around 200 million years ago, Pangaea had split into two smaller masses. Gondwanaland included land that would become the Southern Hemisphere. Laurasia included land that would become most of the Northern Hemisphere.

CONTINENTAL DRIFT

In time, Pangaea split apart and separate landmasses formed. These landmasses eventually became the continents we know today. This theory is now known as continental drift. Over millions of years, the continents have drifted to their current positions. And they are still moving!

Scientists have gathered evidence to support this theory. They have discovered similar fossils on landmasses that are now separated by oceans. They have evidence of glaciers in places where today's climate does not suggest the presence of ice. They are able to show that the continents appear to fit together.

This view of Earth was created from images taken by satellites orbiting our planet. The landmasses we live on today, such as Asia and Africa, took their shapes around ten million years ago.

CONTINENTAL DRIFT: FOSSIL EVIDENCE

The theory of continental drift answered the question of how similar fossils ended up on separate continents. Fossils of a prehistoric reptile called *Mesosaurus* had been found on the southern tips of both South America and Africa. The idea that the continents were once joined explains how this freshwater reptile could be found in these two distant locations.

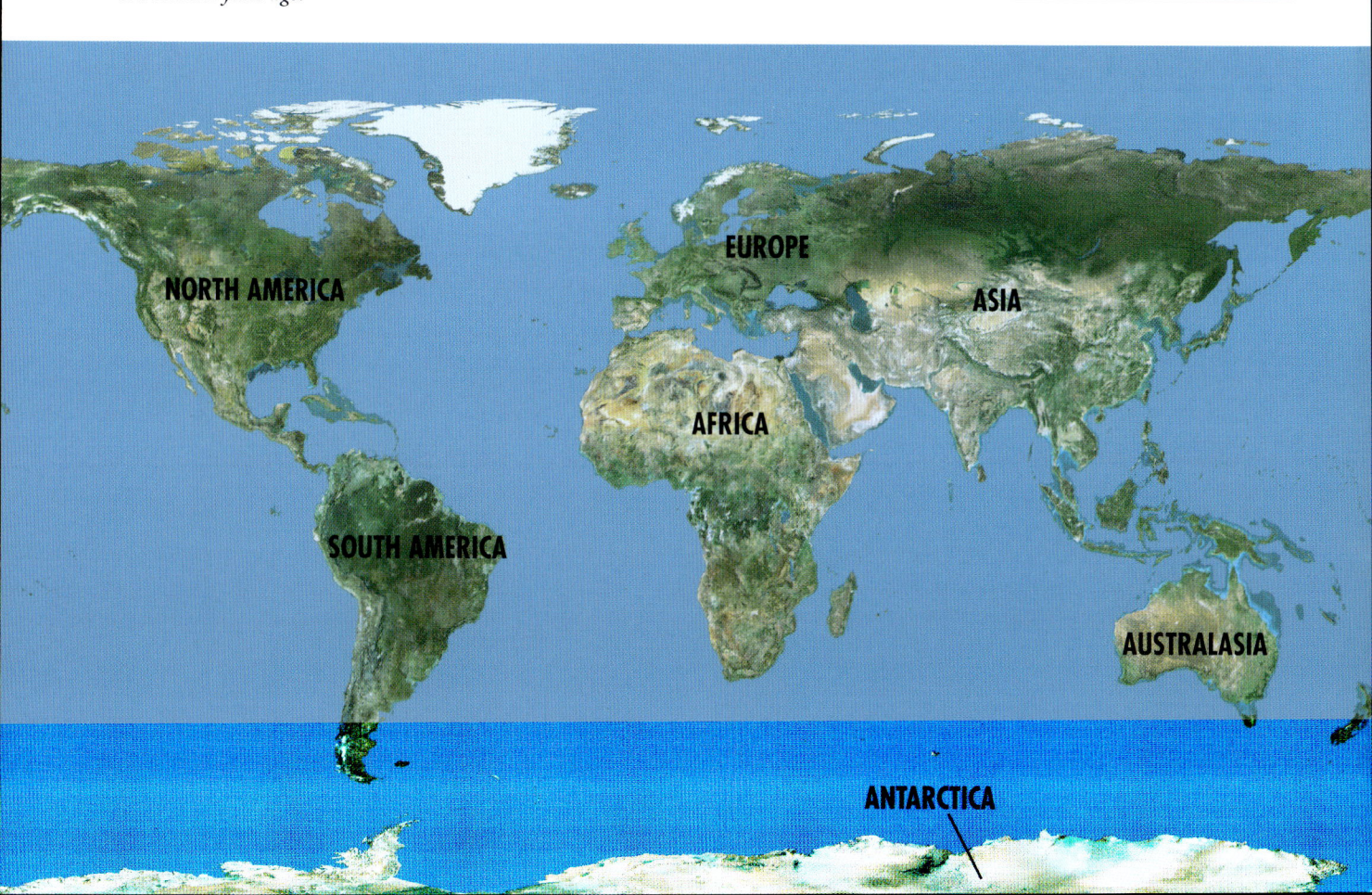

EARTH'S TECTONIC PLATES

Earth's tectonic plates fit together like a giant jigsaw puzzle.

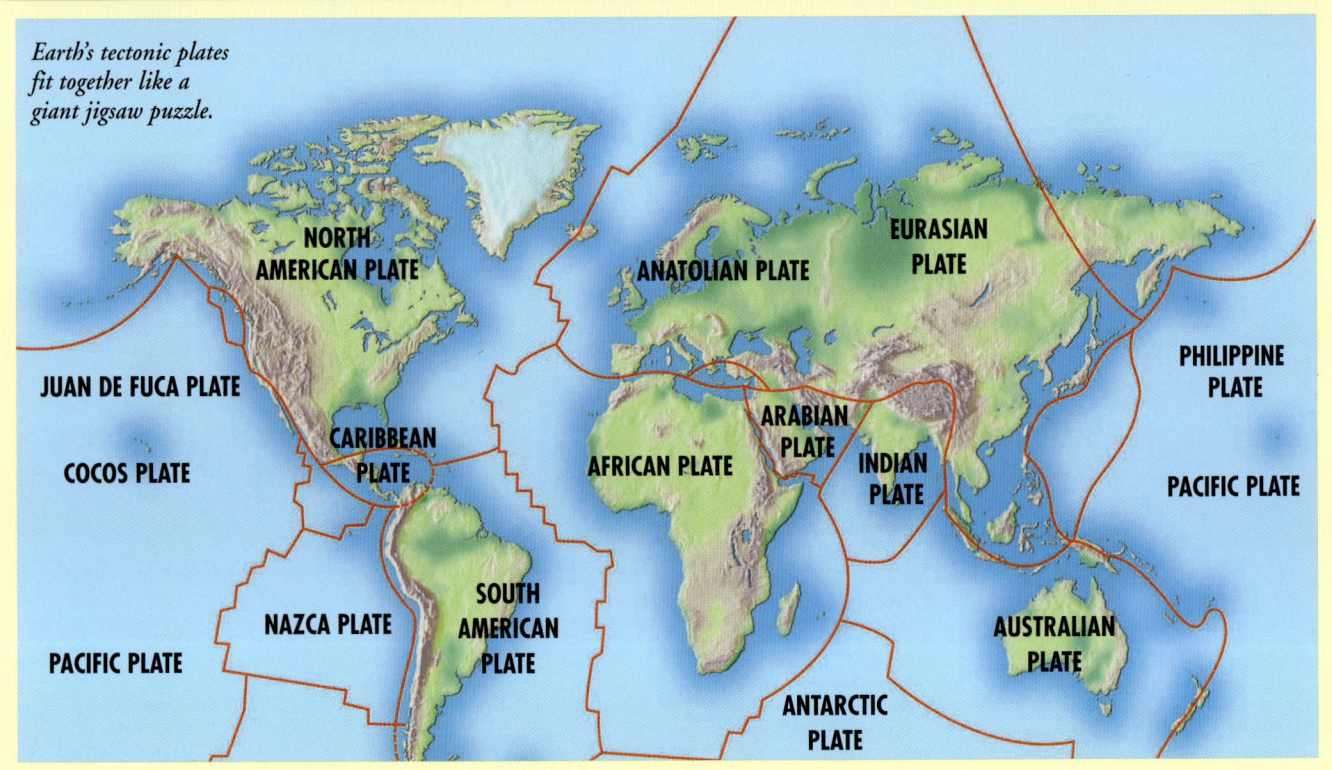

NORTH AMERICAN PLATE
EURASIAN PLATE
ANATOLIAN PLATE
JUAN DE FUCA PLATE
PHILIPPINE PLATE
COCOS PLATE
CARIBBEAN PLATE
ARABIAN PLATE
AFRICAN PLATE
INDIAN PLATE
PACIFIC PLATE
NAZCA PLATE
SOUTH AMERICAN PLATE
PACIFIC PLATE
AUSTRALIAN PLATE
ANTARCTIC PLATE

Today, the continents are still moving. North America and Europe are slowly drifting apart at a rate of around 0.60 in. (1.5cm) each year. The Atlantic and Indian oceans get wider by a few centimeters each year, while the Pacific Ocean is shrinking very slowly.

CITIES ON THE MOVE

SAN ANDREAS FAULT
SAN FRANCISCO
LOS ANGELES
MOVEMENT OF THE NORTH AMERICAN PLATE
MOVEMENT OF THE PACIFIC PLATE

On the West Coast of the United States, two tectonic plates meet along the San Andreas Fault. The two plates are moving past each other at an average rate of around 2 in. (5cm) each year.

In around 11 million years, the cities of San Francisco and Los Angeles in California could be next to each other!

PLATE TECTONICS

What the earlier scientists did not have was knowledge of plate tectonics. Earth's crust and the rigid upper section of the mantle are known together as the lithosphere. The rigid lithosphere is broken up into huge pieces called tectonic plates.

The tectonic plates support the continents and oceans, but they are moving constantly. They float on the oozing liquid mantle below—moving just a few centimeters each year.

Scientists now know that most of the changes in Earth's crust are caused by the movement of the plates in the lithosphere.

FAULTS

As tectonic plates move slowly, they squeeze and stretch rocks under the ground, and an enormous pressure builds up. Sometimes, Earth's crust is put under such great pressure that cracks appear. The places where the crust cracks are called faults.

OUR RESTLESS EARTH

The San Andreas Fault is a 744-mi. (1,200-km)-long fault that runs along the Pacific coast of the U.S.

INSIDE A VOLCANO

A volcano is a mountain made from many layers of lava. Each time it erupts, a new layer is added. Its hollow center provides a path between the mantle and the surface.

The sides of the volcano grow steeper as the lava from each eruption builds up.

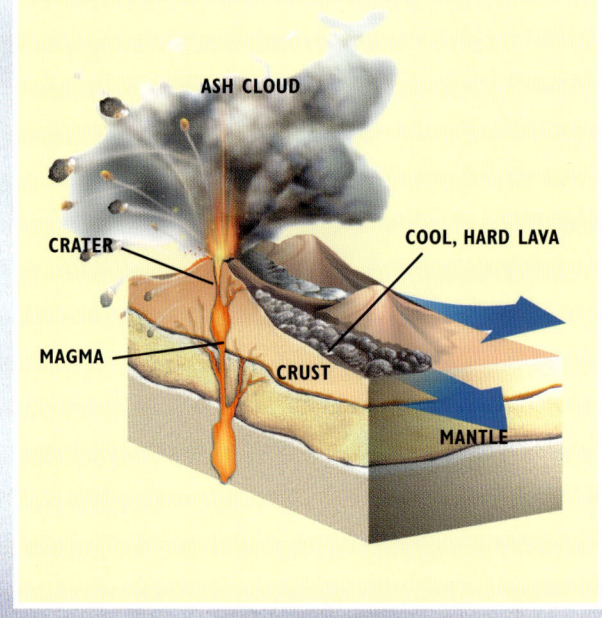

CHAPTER 4: Changing Face of Earth

Very active forces came together to create Earth. Many of those forces continue to affect the planet today. Volcanic eruptions and earthquakes are natural events that affect and shape the planet's surface. They are also signs of activity within the planet's crust, mantle, and core.

VOLCANOES

Earth is dotted with volcanoes. Some are on the land. Some lie under the oceans. Many of Earth's volcanoes occur along the edges of tectonic plates.

EARTH'S RING OF FIRE

Earth has more than 500 active volcanoes. An "active" volcano is one that has erupted in recorded history. This amount does not include the volcanoes in the oceans. Counting them would increase the total. Many volcanoes are located along a path called the Ring of Fire. This very active line of volcanoes is around the boundaries of the Pacific plate. There is also a lot of earthquake activity there.

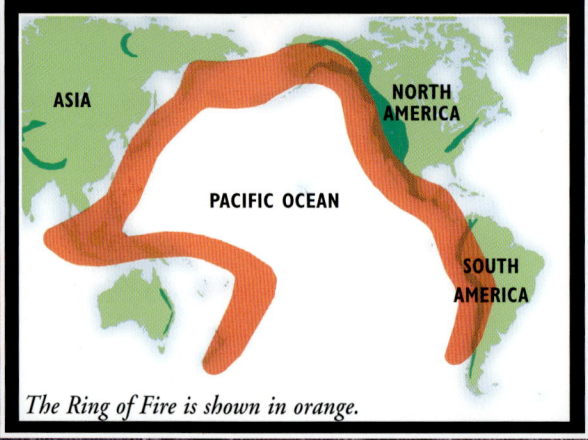

The Ring of Fire is shown in orange.

CHANGING FACE OF EARTH

Some volcanoes erupt along the ocean ridges as plates move apart. Others form where an ocean plate meets a continental plate. But not all form in these ways—some volcanoes simply rise up in the middle of a plate. These are created by hot spots—areas where hot rock from the mantle rises toward Earth's surface.

Volcanoes are of special interest to scientists. A volcano's lava gives scientists a direct look at material from inside our planet. It also gives them evidence of processes taking place miles below Earth's crust.

Sometimes magma breaks through Earth's crust at a hot spot. When this happens under the ocean, it can form an island. Every time the volcano erupts, it grows bigger. One day, if the volcano erupts at the water's surface, it will form a volcanic island. The Hawaiian Islands were created in this way.

IDENTIFYING LAVA

Lava takes different forms. It can be smooth, crumbly, or even formed from big blocky chunks.
The form lava takes depends on:
- what it is made of
- how much gas is in it
- the temperature of the flow

PAHOEHOE FLOW
Lava that looks smooth and ropelike

AA FLOW
Lava that is coarse and sometimes sticky

PILLOW FLOW
Lava that flows under the water

WONDERFUL WORLD

FAULT LINES

During an earthquake, Earth's crust can break along a fault. The rock on both sides of the fault shifts, either sideways or up and down.

NORMAL FAULT
A normal fault occurs when plates diverge, or move away from each other.

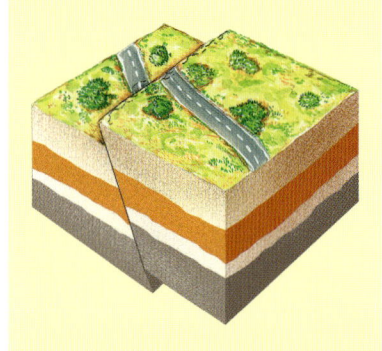

REVERSE FAULT (DIP-SLIP)
A reverse fault occurs when plates converge, or move toward each other.

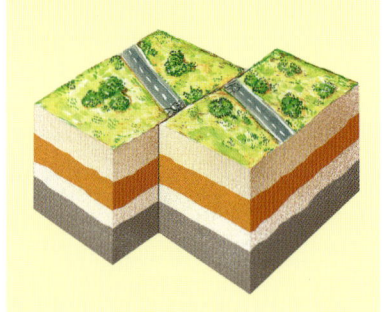

SLIP FAULT (STRIKE-SLIP)
A slip fault occurs when plates move past each other in a horizontal, or side-by-side, path.

EARTHQUAKES

An earthquake begins with a buildup of stress along a fault. The two sides of a fault try to slip past each other, but they get stuck. Stress builds under the ground. The crust bends and flexes. Sometimes the bending and flexing does not relieve the tension. Suddenly, far underground, rocks break and give way. Vibrations called seismic waves are sent out. They make the ground on the surface shake violently—an earthquake!

Rescue workers and survivors search through the rubble of Pisco, Peru, following an earthquake in August 2007.

TSUNAMIS

Earthquakes can occur at faults underwater, too. When they do, this can cause a tsunami—a giant wave. The water absorbs the energy of the earthquake, and waves ripple out from the earthquake's epicenter. The epicenter is the place on Earth's surface directly above where the earthquake starts.

The waves can move out across the ocean as fast as 500 mph (800km/h). At this point, the waves may be small. But as they approach land and move into shallower waters, they slow down and start to grow taller. As deadly tsunami waves hit the shore, they can be 100 ft. (30m) tall!

MOUNTAINS

Mountains are one of Earth's constantly changing features. They are formed when the planet's tectonic plates move. As the plates collide or push against each other, their edges bend out of shape. This causes huge, rocky landforms to appear on Earth's surface—mountains. It can take thousands or millions of years for a mountain to form.

WATER AT WORK

Water is another factor in the constant changes of Earth's surface. Rivers make huge alterations to the landscape. As a river runs its course, it washes away the rock beneath it, and over many years it can carve a deep valley into Earth's crust. An ocean changes the edges of Earth's landmasses. It crashes into the shore and slowly creates craggy cliffs.

The Andes are the world's longest chain of mountains, at 5,500 mi. (8,800km) long. They were formed around 70 million years ago when the Nazca plate collided with the South American plate. The Andes are fold mountains.

MAKING MOUNTAINS

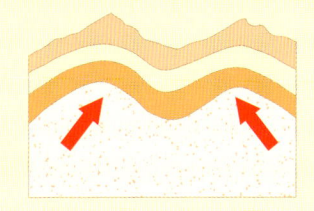

FOLD MOUNTAINS
Plate movements can sometimes force rocks to push against one another, fold, and rise up. Mountains are pushed up at upfolds, and valleys form in downfolds.

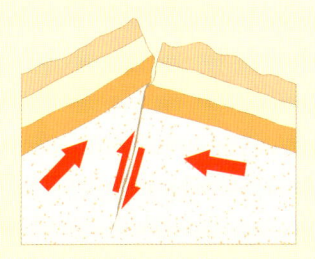

FAULT MOUNTAINS
Sometimes, Earth's surface cracks on a fault. Layers of rock on one side of the fault can be pushed up to form a mountain.

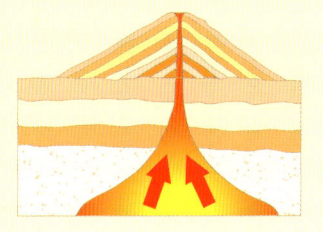

VOLCANIC MOUNTAINS
Some mountains are formed by volcanic activity. Volcanic mountains are made up of lava and rocks. After each volcanic eruption, a new layer of lava hardens and cools.

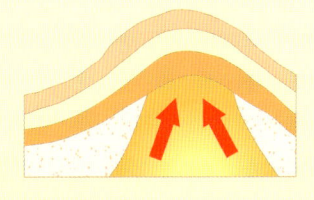

DOME MOUNTAINS
Sometimes heat from inside the mantle pushes Earth's crust upward. This creates a bulge on the surface.

CHAPTER 5:
Earth's Building Materials

Have you ever watched an excavator dig a deep hole in the ground? If it keeps digging down, it will always hit solid rock sooner or later. That's because layers of rock cover the entire surface of our planet.

ROCKS ARE EVERYWHERE

In some parts of Earth's crust, the rocks are really ancient. Rocks have been found in Greenland that are

You can find rocks everywhere, from mountains and riverbanks to beaches and caves.

Layers of rock are hidden under soil, water, and ice.

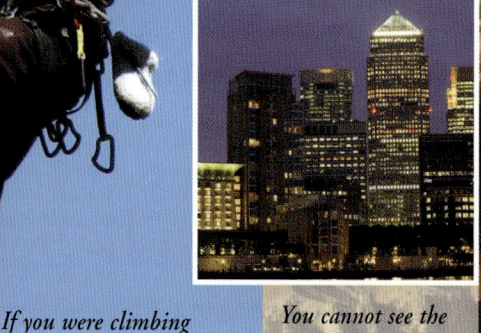

If you were climbing up a cliff, you would be face-to-face with Earth's crust.

You cannot see the rocks below our cities, but they are there!

SOIL

When tiny pieces of rocks mix with the remains of dead plants and animals, soil is created. Different types of rocks create different types of soils. The process of creating soil is speeded up by plant roots. As trees and other plants grow, their roots work themselves into cracks, splitting apart rocks. This plant activity, and animals burrowing in soil, helps break up new soil into smaller and smaller pieces.

EARTH'S BUILDING MATERIALS

more than four billion years old. However, new rocks are forming all the time—right beneath your feet!

EARTH'S ROCKS

There are three main types of rocks on Earth: igneous, sedimentary, and metamorphic. They are all formed in different ways.

This photograph shows Cedar Breaks National Monument in Utah. This vast bowl-shaped limestone cliff extends 2,000 ft. (600m) downward. You can see the different colors and layers of rock that make up Earth's crust.

MAKING ROCKS

IGNEOUS ROCKS
Igneous rocks are those that harden from molten magma or lava. Some igneous rocks form from magma deep within Earth. Others form on Earth's surface. Lava from volcanoes cools and hardens to form igneous rocks. Granite is a type of igneous rock. The giant faces of four U.S. presidents are carved in granite at Mount Rushmore in South Dakota.

SEDIMENTARY ROCKS
Sedimentary rocks are formed from layers of sediment. Over many years, pressure from the layers above and constant heat pack the sediment together. Eventually the layers join and form rocks. You can usually see the layers of sediment in sedimentary rocks. Sandstone is a type of sedimentary rock.

METAMORPHIC ROCKS
Metamorphic rocks are those that have been transformed from one type of rock into another. This happens deep underground. Most metamorphic rocks form because of great heat and pressure deep within Earth. Marble is a type of metamorphic rock.

THE ROCK CYCLE

The rock cycle is a constant process of change. It transforms rocks from one type into another type. It is happening around us and under our feet all the time!

Hot liquid rock (magma) from the mantle is pushed to the surface. This happens when volcanoes erupt or Earth's plates move.

Lava from volcanoes cools on the surface and forms igneous rocks.

Wind, rain, and snow erode rocks.

Rocks from deep underground are brought to the surface by moving plates.

Rivers wash sediment into lakes.

Over a long time, rocks on Earth's surface are worn or washed away. They crumble into smaller and smaller pieces, forming layers of mud or sand called sediment.

Sediment (particles of rock or sand) is buried under more material on land and in water. Over millions of years, it forms new layers of rock called sedimentary rock.

Sedimentary rock is often dragged deep underground by moving plates. It is baked, twisted, and squeezed into metamorphic rock.

WHAT ARE ROCKS MADE FROM?

Rocks are made from substances called minerals. These are solid chemicals that are found in nature. Minerals are inorganic. This means they do not come from plants or animals. However, plants and animals do need certain minerals to survive. You need the calcium in milk for healthy bones. One mineral you probably eat every day is salt. Common table salt is made from the mineral halite.

Like this piece of quartz, a specific mineral always has the same makeup. Each mineral has a definite shape.

EARTH'S BUILDING MATERIALS

WHAT ARE MINERALS?

You probably know more minerals that you realize. Gold, silver, and the gemstones used in jewelry are all minerals. You can also find minerals in everyday objects—such as the graphite in pencils.

Around 3,800 minerals have been found on Earth, but most are rare. Every type of rock has its own unique combination of one or more minerals. For example, pure sandstone is made from only one mineral—quartz. Quartz is one of the most common minerals. Granite is mostly made up of three minerals: feldspar, quartz, and mica.

These table-salt crystals have been magnified using a scanning electron microscope. They are the salt crystals you sprinkle on your food.

WHAT ARE CRYSTALS?

In nature, minerals usually occur in geometrical shapes called crystals. They have smooth faces, straight edges, and symmetrical corners. Halite (table-salt) crystals are shaped like tiny cubes. Zircon crystals are shaped like a pyramid; they are sometimes used in jewelry. Millions of tiny crystals often cluster together to make a chunk of rock. Most gemstones are crystals.

GEMSTONES

Some rare and beautiful minerals are known as gemstones. They are rough when first taken out of the ground, but they sparkle when they have been cut into shapes and polished. Each of these minerals has its own unique shape and color.

A POLISHED SAPPHIRE

AMETHYST CRYSTALS

A RAW OPAL

A POLISHED EMERALD SET IN A RING

A POLISHED DIAMOND SET IN A RING

A RUBY AND DIAMOND BROOCH

Part Two
Earth's Weather and Climate

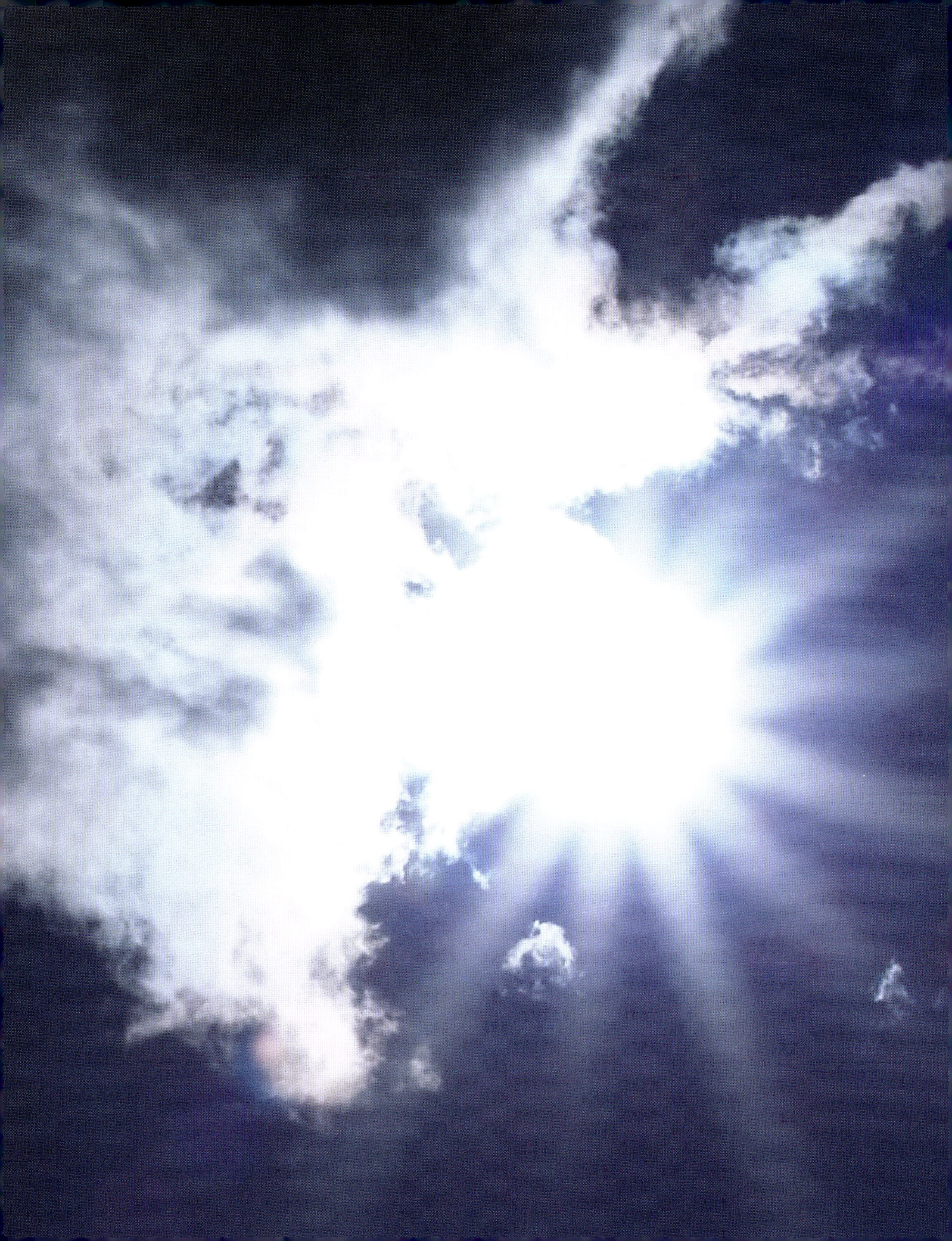

WONDERFUL WORLD

SUN
The Sun's heat is the driving force behind all our weather.

RAIN
Plants rely on rain to bring the water they need for life.

SNOW
Snowflakes form when the temperature drops below freezing.

THUNDERSTORMS
Some dramatic storms produce thunder and lightning.

CHAPTER 6: The World's Weather

Weather and climate affect how you dress, what you eat, and even your vacation plans. The weather can whip up waves at sea and carve out the ground and rocks around us. But watch out! Extreme weather can wipe out entire cities, killing hundreds of people and leaving millions without homes.

WHAT IS WEATHER?

Earth is surrounded by a giant blanket of air called the atmosphere. Weather is what's going on in the atmosphere right above your head. It can also be affected by something that happens thousands of miles away.

WEATHER SURPRISES

Thanks to modern science and technology, weather forecasts are now fairly accurate, but mistakes still happen. On October 16, 1987, no storm was forecast in the U.K. However, the next day, freak hurricane winds battered southern England—knocking down 15 million trees.

THE WORLD'S WEATHER

DISASTERS

Weather creates many of the world's worst disasters. Droughts can cause famine when crops wither and animals starve. Every year, flooding causes thousands of deaths. Weather forecasters try to predict when bad weather will strike—but when a storm rips through a town, we can only run for cover.

In August 2005, Hurricane Katrina caused widespread flooding in New Orleans, Louisiana.

DANGEROUS WEATHER

EXTREME HEAT
If your body's temperature rises by around 7°F (4°C), you may be suffering from heat stroke. Without treatment, it can lead to brain damage or death. Drink plenty of water in the heat.

LOST IN THE FOG
Fog is a cloud that touches the ground. It's difficult to see very far in fog, and it's easy to lose your way. Fog can also be dangerous for people traveling by car or boat.

STUCK IN THE SNOW
Snow has changed history on many occasions. When the French emperor Napoleon attacked Russia in 1812, he was defeated by the fierce Russian winter. Only 20,000 out of his 600,000 men survived the trip home.

Plants and animals have adapted to the weather conditions in the areas where they live. Buffalo in North America grow a thick coat to protect them from the cold during the winter.

WHAT IS CLIMATE?

When a certain type of weather affects a region of Earth most of the time, it is called climate. The world can be divided into areas with different climates (see right).

What's it like where you live? Hopefully not too extreme. Around 40 percent of us live in temperate climates. These are climates in between the cold polar areas and the hot areas near the equator. In temperate climates, there is rainfall throughout the year and the temperature changes with the seasons.

Climate affects which plants and animals are found in an area, but other things—like soil—are also important. The world can also be divided into large regions according to what grows and lives there. These regions are called biomes (see page 57).

The saguaro cactus (left) grows in the Sonoran Desert in the southwestern United States. During a single rainfall, the plant's roots can soak up 198 gal. (750L) of water—enough to last the plant for one year!

THE WORLD'S WEATHER

CLIMATES OF THE WORLD

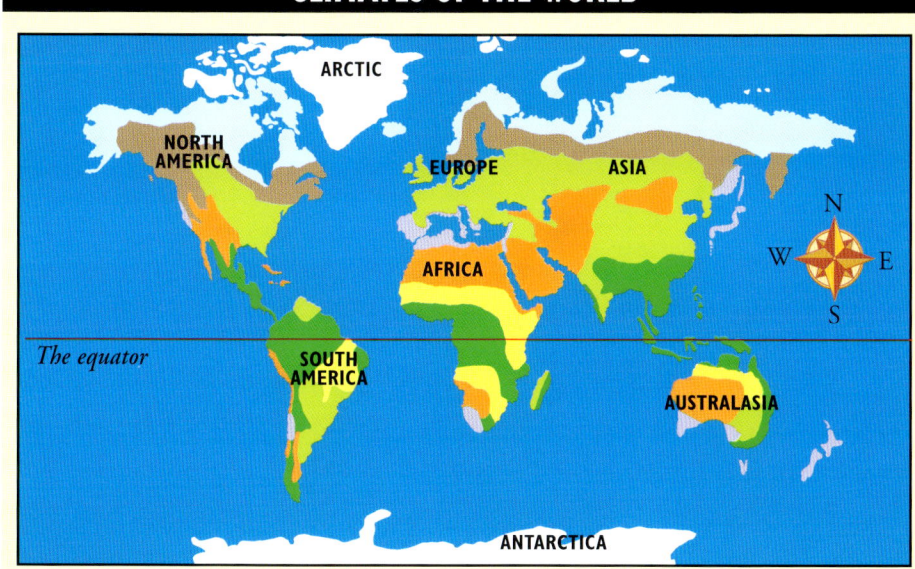

MAP KEY

- **TROPICAL WET** — Hot and wet all year long
- **TEMPERATE** — Warm summers, cool winters, average rainfall
- **DESERT** — Dry land with little rain
- **TUNDRA** — Cold and windy, little rain or snow
- **TROPICAL MONSOON** — Hot all year long, with wet and dry seasons
- **MEDITERRANEAN** — Warm, dry summers, mild winters
- **SUBARCTIC** — Cold winters, cool summers, low rainfall
- **ICECAP** — Extremely cold and dry all year long

HOT IN THE CITY

During the day, buildings are warmed by the air around them. If it is a hot day, they can get quite warm. The materials from which the buildings are made hold onto the heat. After the sun sets, the air begins to cool off. The buildings slowly cool down, giving off, or radiating, the heat they've held. This can make a city up to 10°F (5°C) warmer at night than the temperature in the surrounding countryside.

WHAT GROWS IN THE WORLD'S CLIMATES?

TROPICAL WET
Plenty of rain and sunlight support rainforests, which are home to millions of different plants.

TROPICAL MONSOON
Large areas of grasslands or savannas. A few trees and bushes grow there.

TEMPERATE
Areas of grasslands or forests containing broad-leaved trees such as oaks.

MEDITERRANEAN
Tough grass and small shrubs that can cope with the summer heat.

DESERT
Few plants besides cacti. They survive the dry climate by storing water in their stems.

SUBARCTIC
Large areas of conifer trees. Their dark green leaves absorb the maximum amount of energy from the Sun.

TUNDRA
Plants have shallow roots because below the first few centimeters of ground, the land is frozen.

ICECAP
Land is frozen all year long, so no plants can grow.

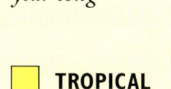

WONDERFUL WORLD

SPRING **SUMMER**

FALL **WINTER**

TEMPERATE SEASONS
In temperate areas, there are four seasons: spring, summer, fall, and winter. The different seasons result in changes for many plants. During the summer, the leaves of broad-leaved trees, such as oaks, use sunlight to make food. During the winter, the shorter days don't provide enough sunlight for them to do this. Losing their leaves saves the trees energy.

THE SUN
The Sun heats our world, warming some parts more than others. This makes the air warmer above these areas. Warm air can't stay still, leading to air movements called convection currents. This moving air is what makes the weather change. The uneven heating of Earth by the Sun also causes water in the air to form clouds, rain, and snow.

THE SEASONS
The Sun also gives us the seasons—the changes in the weather that happen each year at around the same time. Earth takes 365 days, or one year, to orbit the Sun. But it does so tilted at an angle. During the summer, the part of the world where you live tilts toward the Sun, giving days that are warmer and longer. During the winter, it tilts away from the Sun, so the days are colder and shorter.

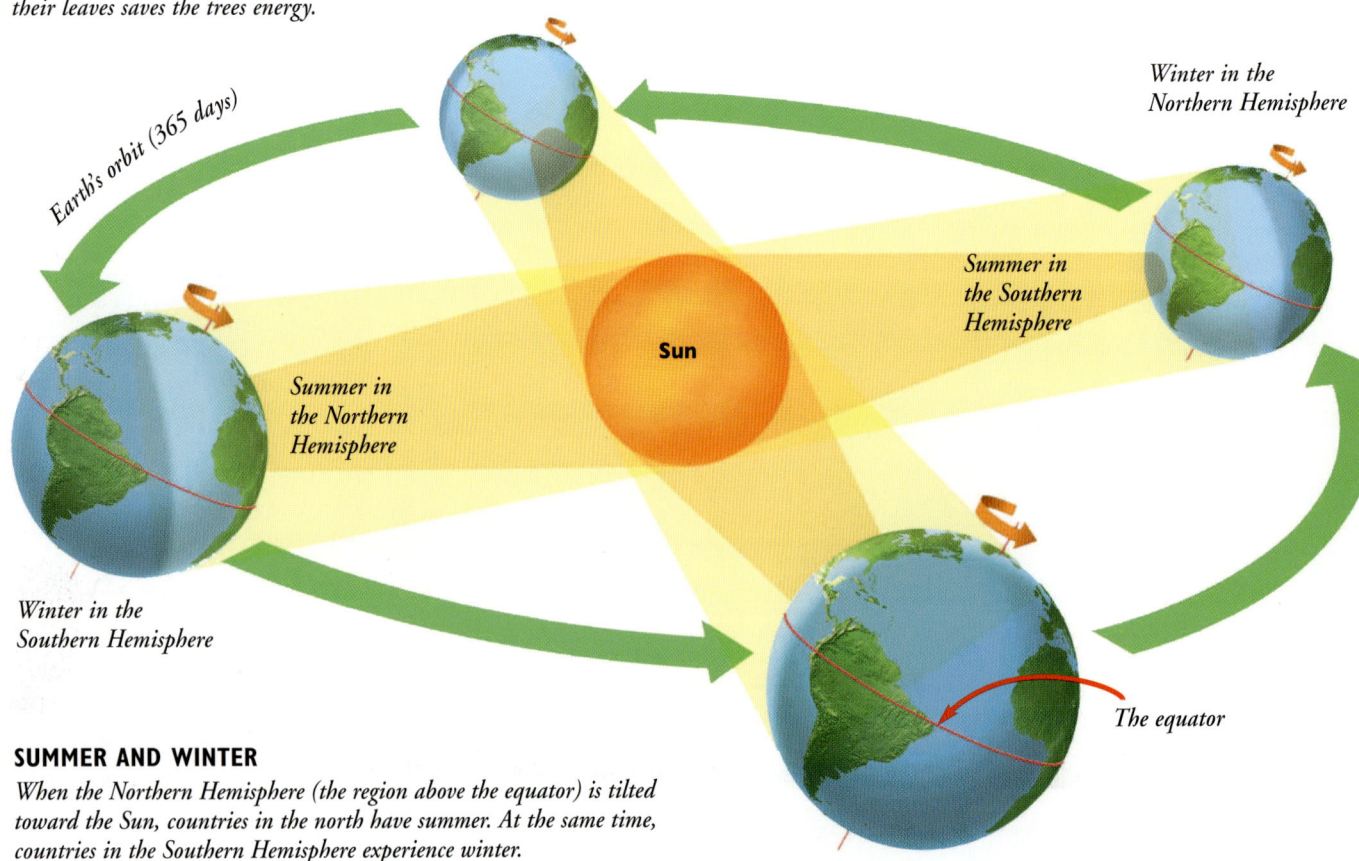

Earth's orbit (365 days)

Winter in the Northern Hemisphere

Summer in the Southern Hemisphere

Sun

Summer in the Northern Hemisphere

Winter in the Southern Hemisphere

The equator

SUMMER AND WINTER
When the Northern Hemisphere (the region above the equator) is tilted toward the Sun, countries in the north have summer. At the same time, countries in the Southern Hemisphere experience winter.

THE WORLD'S WEATHER

TROPICAL MONSOON SEASONS
Near the equator, the weather is hot for most of the year. There are two seasons—a dry season and a rainy, or monsoon, season. These people in Mumbai (Bombay), India, are trying to save their belongings during flooding caused by heavy monsoon rains.

DAY AND NIGHT

As Earth spins around, the Sun seems to move across the sky. This gives us night and day and—you've guessed it—more changes in the weather. In the morning, the Sun rises, warming the ground and the air above the ground. At noon, the Sun is hottest. After the Sun sets, the air cools again.

WONDERFUL WORLD

THE WATER CYCLE

The Sun's heat warms the water in lakes and the oceans. This turns water into an invisible gas called water vapor. The water vapor rises up into the sky. There it cools and turns back into drops of water. The drops fall to the ground as rain or snow. The rain flows into rivers and down into the oceans, where the whole process begins again. This is the water cycle.

Water can create so many types of weather because it is able to turn easily from a liquid to a gas—it can evaporate. The amount of water that falls as rain and snow is exactly the same as the amount that evaporates.

The water on our planet gets used over and over again. The raindrops falling on your head contain the same water that fell on the dinosaurs more than 65 million years ago.

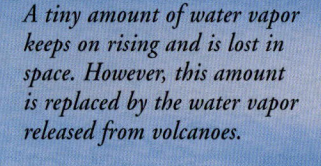

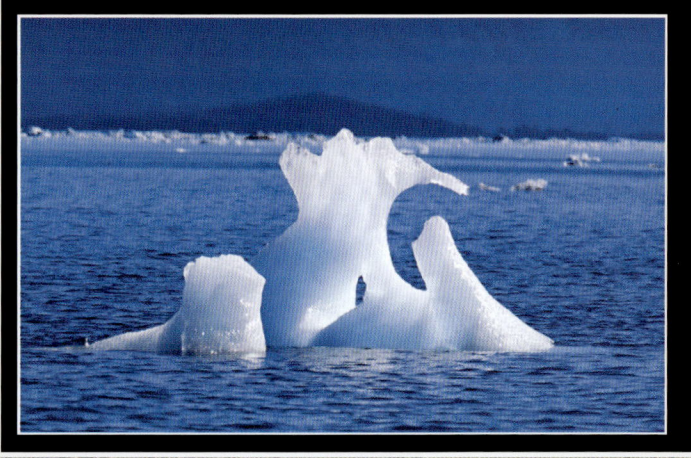

A tiny amount of water vapor keeps on rising and is lost in space. However, this amount is replaced by the water vapor released from volcanoes.

POLAR ICE

When it gets very cold, water turns into solid ice. Most of the world's ice is found at the poles, and there's a lot of it! Antarctica is bigger than Europe and is covered in ice that is almost 1 mi. (1.5km) thick. Water held in the form of ice can't go through the rest of the water cycle unless the ice melts.

If global warming causes the ice at the poles to melt, that water will be added to what is already in the oceans. Areas near the sea will be flooded.

THE WORLD'S WEATHER

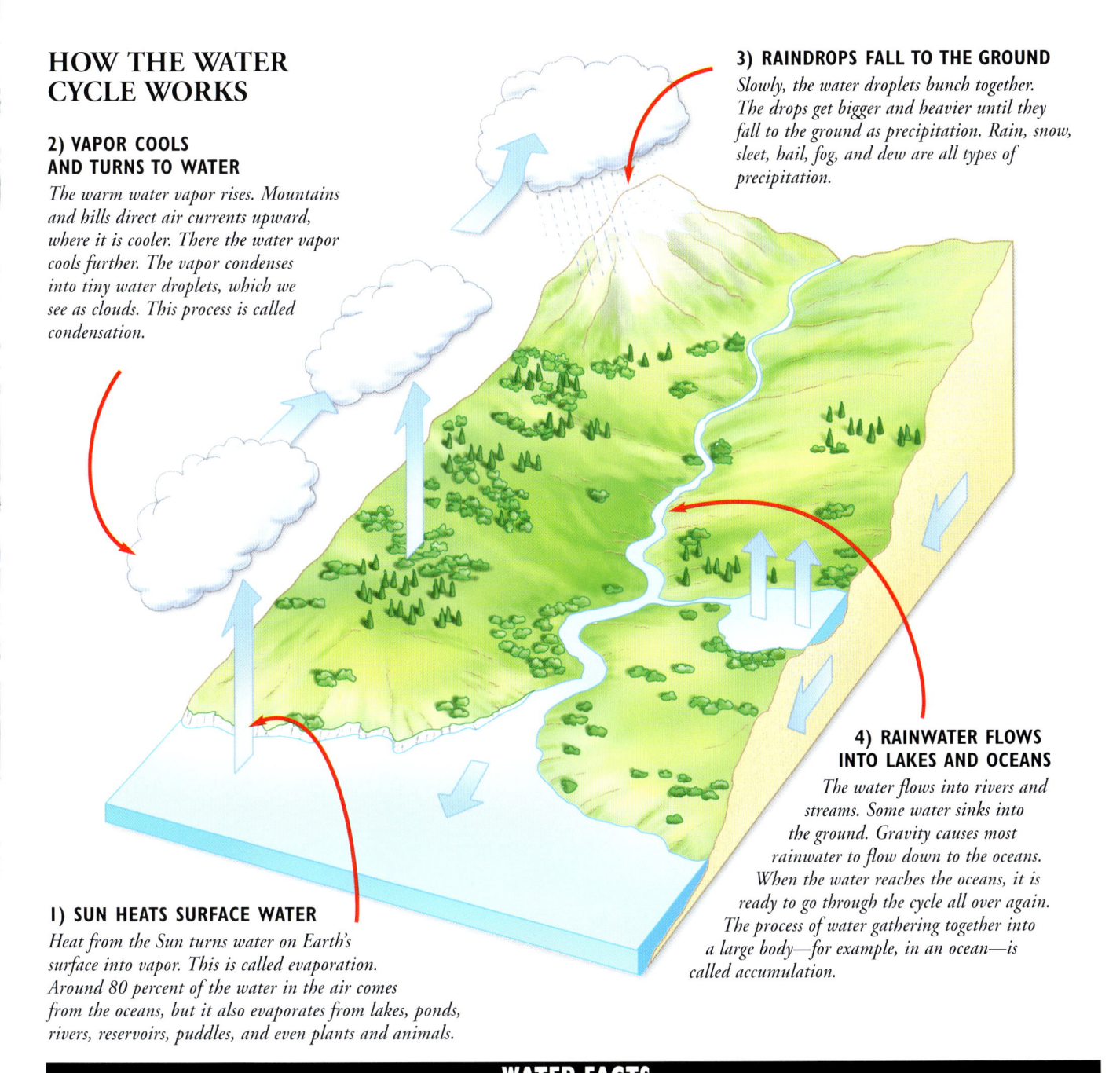

HOW THE WATER CYCLE WORKS

2) VAPOR COOLS AND TURNS TO WATER
The warm water vapor rises. Mountains and hills direct air currents upward, where it is cooler. There the water vapor cools further. The vapor condenses into tiny water droplets, which we see as clouds. This process is called condensation.

3) RAINDROPS FALL TO THE GROUND
Slowly, the water droplets bunch together. The drops get bigger and heavier until they fall to the ground as precipitation. Rain, snow, sleet, hail, fog, and dew are all types of precipitation.

4) RAINWATER FLOWS INTO LAKES AND OCEANS
The water flows into rivers and streams. Some water sinks into the ground. Gravity causes most rainwater to flow down to the oceans. When the water reaches the oceans, it is ready to go through the cycle all over again. The process of water gathering together into a large body—for example, in an ocean—is called accumulation.

1) SUN HEATS SURFACE WATER
Heat from the Sun turns water on Earth's surface into vapor. This is called evaporation. Around 80 percent of the water in the air comes from the oceans, but it also evaporates from lakes, ponds, rivers, reservoirs, puddles, and even plants and animals.

WATER FACTS

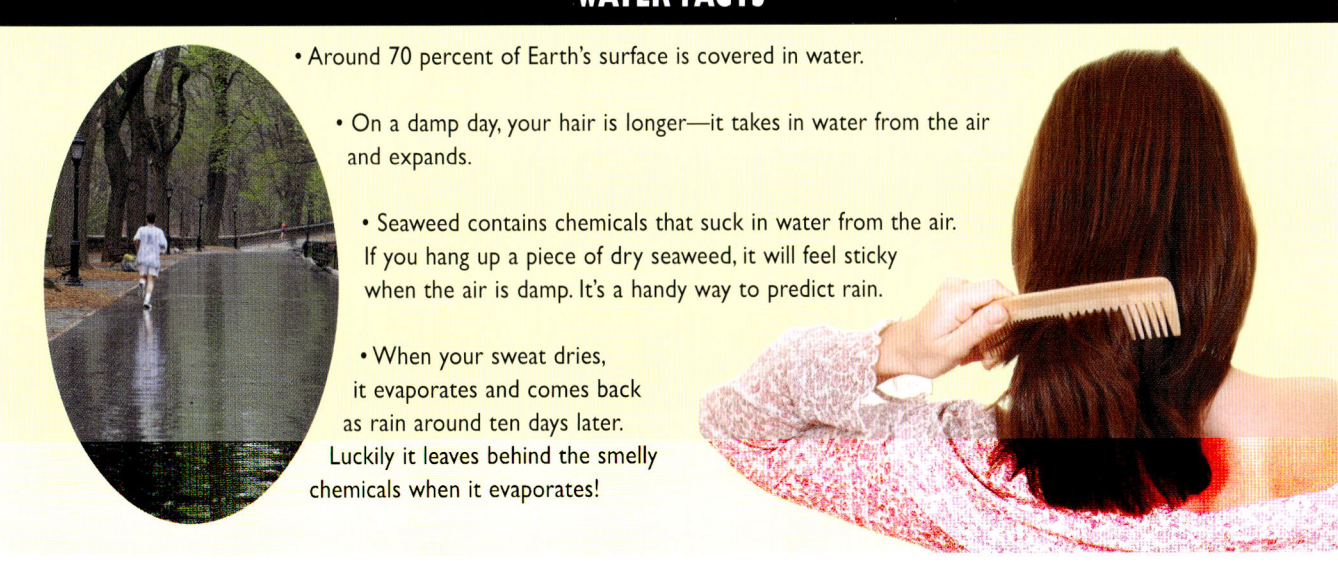

- Around 70 percent of Earth's surface is covered in water.

- On a damp day, your hair is longer—it takes in water from the air and expands.

- Seaweed contains chemicals that suck in water from the air. If you hang up a piece of dry seaweed, it will feel sticky when the air is damp. It's a handy way to predict rain.

- When your sweat dries, it evaporates and comes back as rain around ten days later. Luckily it leaves behind the smelly chemicals when it evaporates!

WONDERFUL WORLD

LAYERS OF THE ATMOSPHERE

THE EXOSPHERE
This layer begins 300 mi. (500km) above Earth's surface. The exosphere is the thin uppermost layer where our atmosphere merges into space.

THE THERMOSPHERE
50–300 mi. (80–500km) above Earth's surface. The International Space Station orbits Earth in the thermosphere.

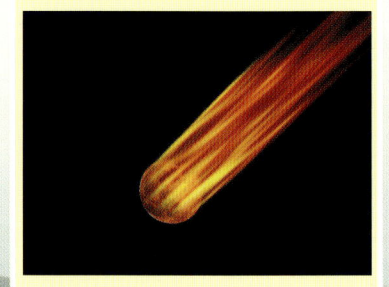

THE MESOSPHERE
30–50 mi. (50–80km) above Earth's surface. Millions of meteors bump into Earth's atmosphere every day and burn up in the mesosphere. You see them as shooting stars.

THE STRATOSPHERE
6–30 mi. (10–50km) above Earth's surface. The stratosphere contains the ozone layer, which cuts out most of the Sun's dangerous rays.

THE TROPOSPHERE
Up to 6 mi. (10km) above Earth's surface. This is the place where almost all weather happens.

CHAPTER 7:
Everyday Weather

Have you ever had to fasten your seat belt on a plane? The bumps you can feel are turbulence—pockets of air moving around. They're part of a giant weather machine that stretches around the whole planet. This machine is driven by the Sun's energy and the oceans, which store a lot of heat (like a huge hot-water bottle).

AIR MASSES
The Sun and oceans heat up some places more than others, so the air in these areas is wetter and warmer than air elsewhere. Giant bodies of this warm, wet air, called air masses, are always on the move—changing the weather where you live.

The proportion of gases in the atmosphere changes as you go higher. Mountain climbers have to cope with altitude sickness caused by less oxygen on mountains more than 10,000 ft. (3,000m) high.

If they didn't spread the Sun's heat around, the hot places would get hotter and the cold places would freeze. In fact, nothing could live on Earth—including you!

FLYING HIGH

The atmosphere is a mixture of gases made up of five layers. Together, the layers stretch 560 mi. (900km) into space. Weather happens only in the layer closest to Earth—the troposphere. Airplanes going on long trips fly right at the top of the troposphere, above the clouds. This helps them avoid turbulence.

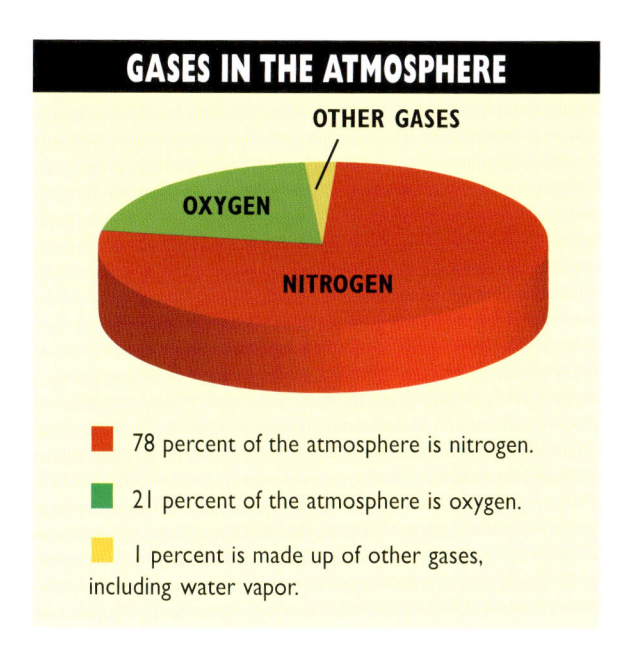

GASES IN THE ATMOSPHERE

- 78 percent of the atmosphere is nitrogen.
- 21 percent of the atmosphere is oxygen.
- 1 percent is made up of other gases, including water vapor.

BLOWING HOT AND COLD

When the Sun heats up the ground, this in turn heats up the air above it. The warm air expands and becomes less dense, allowing it to rise upward. Up in the atmosphere, the warm air cools. It becomes more dense, and gravity causes it to move back down to the ground again. This nonstop movement of warm and cold air sets up a cycle known as convection.

A WORLD OF WIND

JET STREAMS
World War II pilots flying high sometimes found themselves going nowhere because of high-speed winds (up to 250 mph/400km/h) blowing in the opposite direction. Today, pilots try to fly in the direction of jet streams. This gives the planes extra speed and saves fuel.

SEA BREEZES
During the summer, cool breezes blow inland from the ocean. The land is warmer than the ocean, and as warm air rises above the land, cool air rushes in from the ocean to take its place.

WINDS THAT FREEZE
The stronger the wind, the more quickly your body loses heat. This is known as the wind-chill factor. Every extra 1 mi. (2km) per hour of wind speed means your body drops 2°F (1°C) in temperature.

PREVAILING WINDS
Winds that tend to blow in the same direction are called prevailing winds. Trade winds blow from east to west across the Atlantic Ocean. These reliable winds helped early European traders sail to the Americas.

WIND

There's more than five million billion tons of air in the atmosphere. In fact, all the air pressing down on your head and shoulders weighs around one ton—the same weight as a car! Air pressure squeezes your whole body, but you don't get crushed because of the the air pressure inside your body.

When the warmth from the Sun or the oceans heats the air, this causes differences in air pressure. It makes air masses move around, which is what you feel as wind on the ground.

A strong wind can make it difficult to stand up—it can also give you a very bad hair day!

EVERYDAY WEATHER

Tiny grains of sand carried by the wind can wear away rocks. This erosion may create strange shapes.

IN A SPIN

The world's winds move in a set way around the globe. Hot air near the equator heats up, rises, and moves toward the cold poles. Cold air at the poles moves toward the equator. This is an example of convection at work.

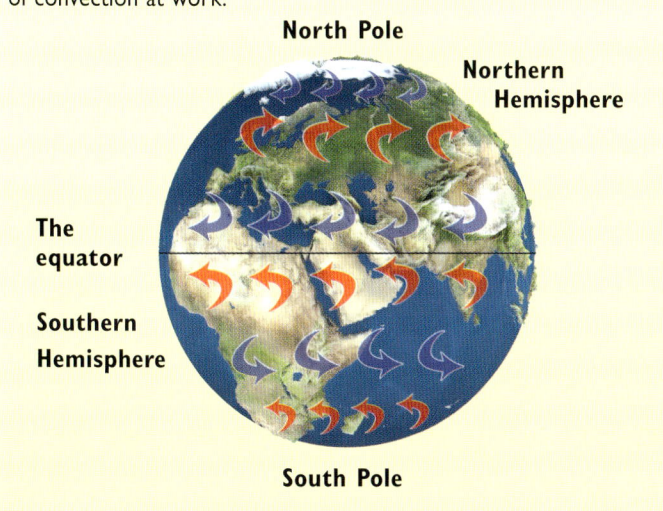

However, the spin of Earth makes these air masses curve and spin, too. Winds rotate counterclockwise in the Northern Hemisphere and clockwise in the Southern Hemisphere. This is known as the Coriolis effect.

MOVING AIR PRESSURE

Think of how a balloon whizzes around when you let out the air. The air inside moves from an area of high pressure (inside the balloon) to an area of low pressure (outside the balloon).

In the atmosphere, when warm air rises, it forms an area of low pressure. Cold air, which is denser, sinks down, creating high pressure. When the pressure is high, the weather is usually sunny. Low pressure often brings rainy or snowy days.

CLOUD GALLERY

NIMBOSTRATUS
A familiar blanket of low, dark rain clouds—expect a steady downpour!

STRATOCUMULUS
A big sheet of low-lying clouds with a more lumpy shape than nimbostratus.

CUMULONIMBUS
Brace yourself—these storm clouds stretch high up into the atmosphere, often bringing heavy rain and lightning.

CLOUDS

As they float across the sky, clouds look as light as a feather. Don't be fooled, though—an average cloud weighs as much as a jumbo jet! Luckily for us, this weight is spread out, so rising warm air keeps a cloud aloft. Clouds are made up of millions of tiny droplets of water or ice, which are so small that they can float in the air.

Clouds form when warm air rises. High up in the sky, the invisible water vapor cools and turns into water droplets. A cloud's shape and height can help you predict the weather.

Clouds form at many different levels. We call clouds that hang close to the ground mist or fog. Some clouds are as high as 39,000 ft. (12,000m) above the ground—higher than Mount Everest.

BAD AIR DAY

City smog is a human-made weather condition. The term *smog* was first used in London, England, in the early 1900s to describe a mixture of smoke and fog. Smog is caused by pollution from vehicle exhausts, power plants, and factories reacting with sun and heat. This produces the thick haze we sometimes see hanging over our cities. Smog can make it difficult to see, but it also causes health problems, from stinging eyes to severe breathing difficulties.

CUMULUS
Fluffy white clouds often seen floating across the sky. Enjoy the good weather!

ALTOCUMULUS
Round clouds in patches—a sign of unsettled weather to come.

CIRRUS
High, wispy white clouds that look like cotton candy. Often the first clouds to form along a weather front.

FRONTS

When two giant air masses bump into each other, they take awhile to mix. A boundary forms between them, known as a front. Clouds often form where a warm air mass meets a cold air mass.

THUNDERSTORMS

The air whizzing around inside a storm cloud can create lightning. This is a huge surge of static electricity that leaps from the bottom of the cloud to the ground. As the lightning rushes through the air, it produces a shock wave that you hear as thunder. Thunderstorms are most common in tropical rainforest areas. In temperate regions, they are most frequent during the summer.

Lightning is hot stuff. The air around a lightning bolt reaches an incredible 59,400ºF (33,000ºC) when it strikes!

Lightning causes many forest fires each year. This is one of nature's ways of clearing dead leaves and overgrown areas. Some plants, such as the bishop pine, actually need intense heat in order for their seeds to sprout.

RAIN CHECK

DOWNPOUR
During a storm, more than 1 in. (3cm) of rain can fall in 15 minutes. At any moment, there are around 2,000 thunderstorms going on somewhere in the world.

MONSOON
In tropical regions, such as India and Southeast Asia, there is a rainy season and a dry season. These can cause floods and then droughts. In 2005, monsoon rains killed 1,000 people in Mumbai (Bombay), India, when 37 in. (94cm) of rain fell in only 24 hours.

ACID RAIN
Acid rain occurs when poisonous gases, such as sulfur dioxide from power plants and cars, combine with water in the air. Acid rain eats away at stone buildings and poisons trees, rivers, and lakes.

RAIN
By the time clouds form, water is well on its way to becoming rain. The tiny water droplets in a cloud cluster together to form bigger drops. When the drops get too heavy, they fall to the ground. It takes around one million cloud droplets to make one raindrop. But all those raindrops add up. Enough rain falls on Earth every day to fill several hundred bathtubs of water for every person on the planet!

When you face a rainbow, the Sun is behind you, directly opposite the rainbow. If you try to chase the rainbow, it seems to be moving with you. You will always be between the Sun and the rainbow!

FREAKY RAIN
Strong air currents have been known to sweep frogs, spiders, fish, and even turtles and snakes up into the air. In August 1918, hundreds of tiny fish fell in Sunderland, U.K., during a thunderstorm.

EVERYDAY WEATHER   47

Ice crystals in very thin cirrus clouds can cause coronas (bright rings) around the Sun and Moon.

WHAT TYPE OF RAIN?
Raindrops come in different shapes and sizes. Drizzle is a fairly steady light rain with raindrops that are around 0.5 millimeters across. The raindrops that fall in a heavy downpour can be up to eight millimeters across.

CHASING RAINBOWS
Rain and sunshine can combine in the most beautiful way. The Sun's white light is actually made up of different colors: red, orange, yellow, green, blue, indigo, and violet. A rainbow is caused by light rays from the Sun being separated into these colors when they pass through raindrops or rain spray.

ICY DANGERS

GIANT HAILSTONE
During a violent hailstorm in June 2003, the largest hailstone in U.S. history fell on Aurora, Nebraska. The hailstone had a circumference of 18.6 in. (47.6cm). It has been preserved at the National Center for Atmospheric Research in Boulder, Colorado.

FREEZING RAIN
When the Great Ice Storm struck Canada in January 1998, heavy rain followed by frost made electric cables snap under the weight of the ice. Four million people were left without electricity in the middle of winter.

WHITEOUT
During whiteouts, the air is so thick with snow you can't tell the ground from the sky. People can lose their sense of direction. Airplanes may crash and birds fly into the ground. Sudden blizzards have even buried trains under heavy snow.

SNOW

When you complain about the cold, remember that 20,000 years ago, most of North America and Europe were covered in a layer of ice almost 2 mi. (3km) thick. The world has warmed up since then, but very cold weather still brings all kinds of hazards.

When the air temperature drops below freezing, water droplets turn into ice crystals. As more water then freezes on the ice crystals, they grow bigger. Then as these crystals tumble down through the clouds, they knock into other crystals and form snowflakes.

If the ground temperature is above freezing, snowflakes start to melt as they fall, turning to sleet.

Frost is water vapor in the air that turns into ice crystals when the temperature drops below 32ºF (0ºC). It forms an icy layer on the ground that can kill plants.

EVERYDAY WEATHER

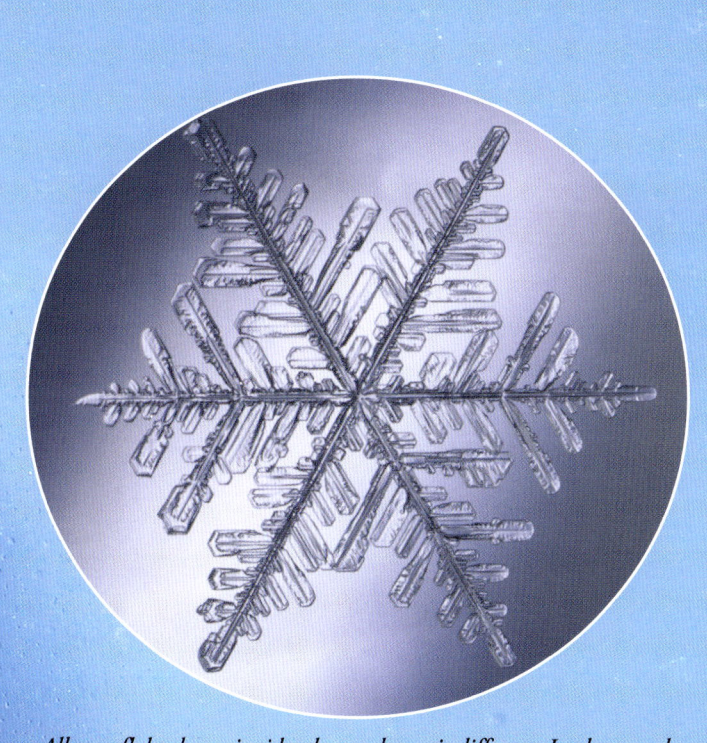

All snowflakes have six sides, but each one is different. Its shape and size depends on the temperature and the amount of moisture in the cloud. The largest snowflakes are around 2 in. (5cm) across.

HAILSTONES

Most hailstones are the size of a pea, but they can be the size of a golf ball—or bigger! A hailstone forms when an updraft carries a water droplet above the freezing level in a storm. The droplet freezes into ice. The tiny hailstone starts to drop down, but then an updraft takes it back up again and it gets coated with another layer of ice. This keeps happening until the hailstone gets too heavy to rise up and it falls from the sky. If you chop a hailstone in half, you can count the layers of ice.

STORM FILE

DESERT WHIRLWINDS
Dust devils are small whirlwinds that often occur in deserts. They are mostly harmless, and many are only a few feet high.

WATER TORNADOES
Waterspouts are tornadoes that occur over water. Some are more than 330 ft. (100m) wide. Like all tornadoes, waterspouts last only a few minutes.

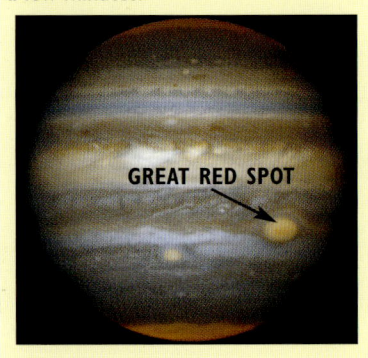

GREAT RED SPOT

STORMS IN SPACE
Earth is not the only planet in the solar system that has storms. The Great Red Spot on Jupiter is a massive storm up to 15,500 mi. (25,000km) across. It has been raging for at least 300 years.

CHAPTER 8:
Extreme Weather

Most of the weather we experience is fairly ordinary: it's sunny, cloudy, rainy, or snowy. But once in awhile, parts of the world experience severe weather. Hurricanes, tornadoes, and floods cause massive destruction and lead to many deaths each year.

HURRICANES

A hurricane starts life as an ordinary tropical storm. Then heat from the ocean warms the air further. Warm, wet air rises rapidly, sucking in more air. The spin of Earth causes the storm to spiral upward around a center, called the eye. When the rising air cools, it creates huge rain clouds. Hurricane winds of up to 155 mph (250km/h) can flatten houses, and the heavy rains lead to flooding.

EXTREME WEATHER

NAME THAT STORM

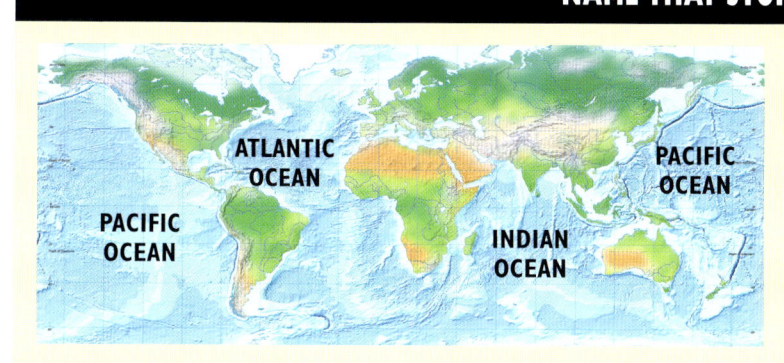

Giant tropical storms have different names depending on where in the world they form.

- Giant storms in the Pacific Ocean are called typhoons.
- Giant storms are known as hurricanes in the Atlantic Ocean.
- In the Indian Ocean, giant storms are known as cyclones.

TORNADOES

Smaller, but equally scary, are tornadoes—vicious funnel-shaped storms that spin down from thunderclouds. The largest tornadoes are around 0.6 mi. (1km) wide, and their winds can reach speeds of 300 mph (480km/h). Thankfully, they last only a few minutes.

A big hurricane can be as large as Australia and up to 6 mi. (10km) high. This satellite image shows Hurricane Katrina, approaching Louisiana in 2005.

TORNADOES

Tornadoes begin when air inside a thundercloud starts to spin. The whirling air spins faster and faster and sucks warm air up from the ground. The warm air cools and forms a spinning funnel-shaped cloud. When the cloud touches the ground, the tornado sets off at speeds of up to 60 mph (100km/h). It smashes everything in its path and can even lift trees many feet into the air.

EXTREME WEATHER RECORD BREAKERS

HOTTEST TEMPERATURE
In 1922, the temperature in Al'Aziziyah, Libya, reached 136°F (58°C).

COLDEST TEMPERATURE
The coldest temperature ever documented was −128.2°F (−89.2°C). This was recorded at Vostok Research Station, Antarctica, in 1983.

WETTEST PLACE
Cherrapunji, India, is one of the wettest places on Earth. It receives an annual rainfall of around 37.7 ft. (11.5m), due to the monsoon rains. Once it rained almost 30 ft. (9m) in one month!

DRIEST PLACE
The Atacama Desert in Chile spreads for 23,300 sq. mi. (80,000km^2). There has never been any rainfall recorded in some parts of this desert.

STRONGEST WIND
The highest nontornado wind gust ever was recorded on Mount Washington in the U.S. on April 12, 1934. It blew at 231 mph (372km/h).

FLOODS

The heavy rain that falls during a storm often causes more damage than the wind. Floods sweep across the ground, washing away crops, vehicles, and even houses. In 1887, the Huang He (Yellow River) in China burst its banks. Around two million people died. Many were drowned, while others died from starvation and disease after the disaster. Heavy floods also result from ocean waves called storm surges, pushed onshore by an advancing hurricane.

Sometimes when rain falls hard and fast, the ground cannot soak up the water fast enough. This is called a flash flood.

In 2005, hundreds of people were killed by a mudslide in the village of Panabaj, Guatemala. Days of torrential rain following a hurricane caused tons of mud to crash down the slopes of the volcano, burying the village.

EXTREME WEATHER

MUDSLIDES

Torrential rains can also cause a massive flow of mud—a mudslide. Sometimes the ground becomes so saturated that it cannot hold any more water. If the saturated ground is on a slope, the overflow rushes downhill, sweeping away anything in its path.

DROUGHTS

Around the world, different areas get different amounts of rain. But sometimes an area will suffer from a drought, receiving less rain than usual—or no rain at all. Without enough rain, people and their animals have no drinking water and crops cannot grow. This can lead to a famine.

During a drought, wild animals may die from a lack of food and water. Dry, cracked soil can be whipped up into dust storms, and dry plants and trees are in danger of catching on fire.

DUST STORMS

During a large storm, clouds of fine dust may be lifted to heights of almost 2 mi. (3km) and then carried for thousands of miles. Sandstorms, such as the haboob in the Middle East and Africa, can move entire sand dunes. These vast walls of dust can strip the paint off a car!

Part Three
Earth's Ecosystems

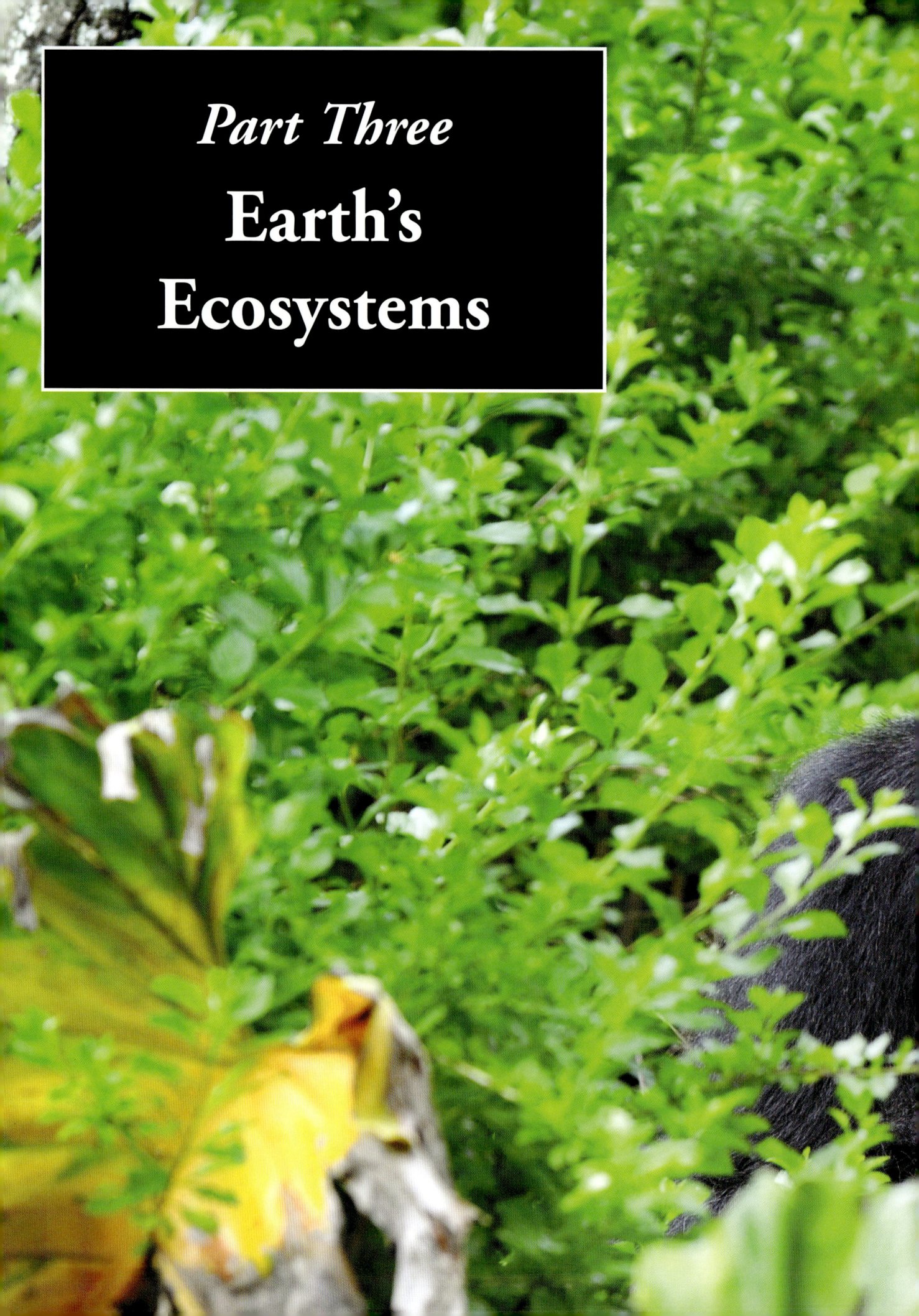

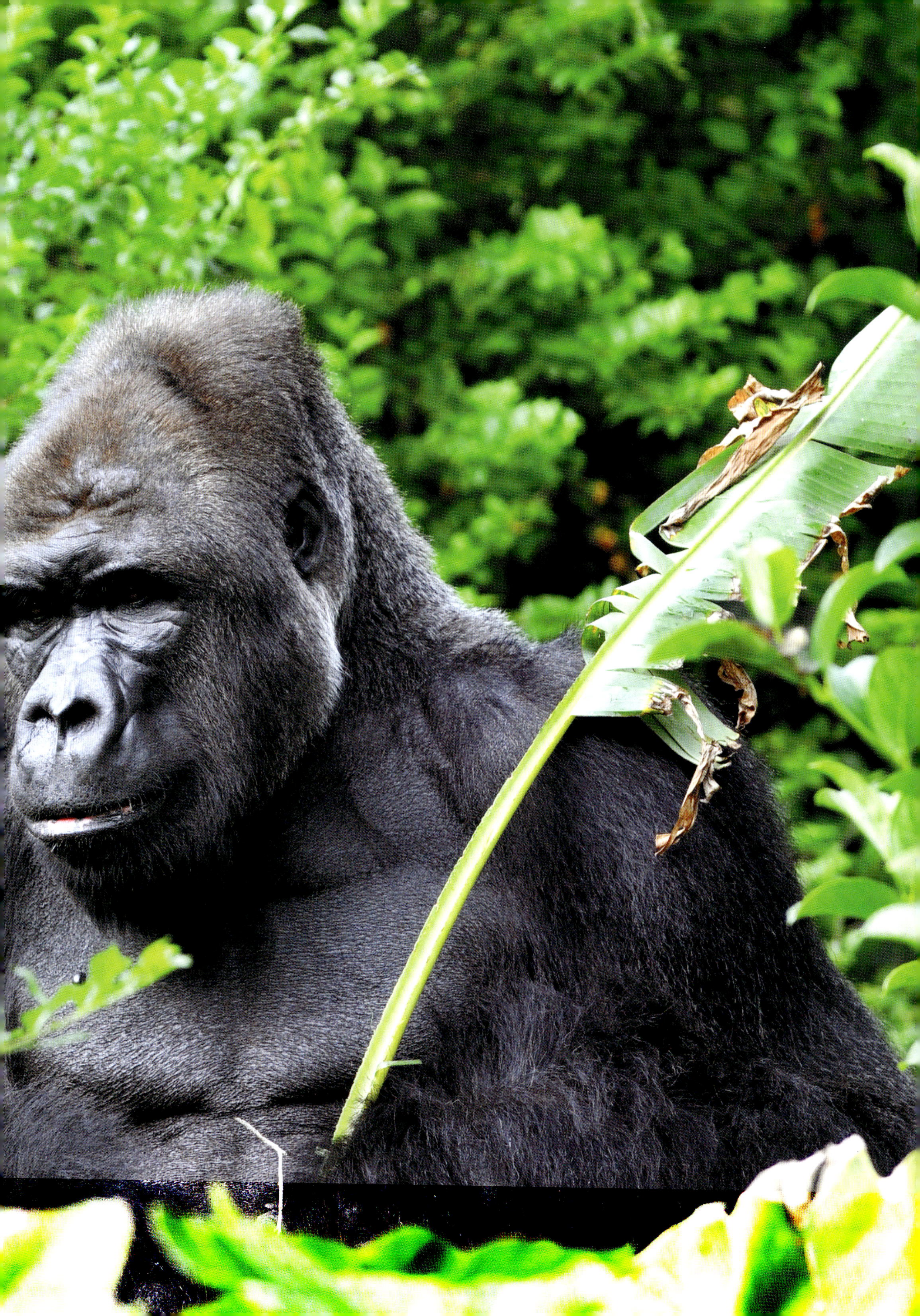

CHAPTER 9:
What Is an Ecosystem?

An ecosystem is a community of living things that rely on one another to survive in a certain environment (the place in which they live). Your home is a type of ecosystem. Your family and pets depend on one another, and the house itself, to supply food, water, and shelter.

ECOSYSTEMS

An ecosystem supports a community, or group, of living things. The different plants and animals in an ecosystem depend on one another to survive. They also depend on nonliving things around them such as soil and water. Ecosystems can be enormous, like the Sahara Desert, or small, like a pond.

Your body is a small ecosystem. Inside you there are thousands of tiny organisms. These include the bacteria that help you digest your food.

A forest is a large ecosystem with many plants and animals.

A single oak tree in the forest can be an ecosystem all of its own.

In the oak tree there is a community of birds, beetles, worms, and fungi (above).

WHAT IS A HABITAT?

The word *habitat* refers to the place where a plant or animal lives. For example, a fish and a mud worm may be part of the same river ecosystem. However, the fish's habitat is the water in the river, while the worm's habitat is the mud flat alongside the river.

WHAT IS A BIOME?

Scientists divide Earth into large areas called biomes (see Chapter 12). A biome is a region with the same climate and similar plants and animals. Each biome contains living things that are suited to the heat, soil, and water in that region. Every type of biome on our planet is found in many parts of the world. Within any one biome, there are many ecosystems made up of smaller communities of plants and animals.

Savannas are a type of biome found in South America and Africa. The African savanna is home to many types of wildlife and has many ecosystems. Here, a pride of lions watches a herd of zebras—their source of food. The lions and zebras are both members of the same ecosystem.

EXAMPLES OF BIOMES

POLAR REGIONS
Polar regions make up one type of biome. They are very cold, windy, and dry. Almost no plants can survive there. Animals such as polar bears, seals, and penguins get their food from the sea.

MOUNTAIN REGIONS
Mountain regions make up another biome. Mountains are cold, windy, and wet. Past a certain height, it is so cold that trees will not grow. This height is called the timberline.

DESERTS
Deserts make up a biome that is very hot and dry. Desert plants and animals can survive on very little water. Desert temperatures are cooler at night, when desert animals are more active.

Light and heat from the Sun . . .   *. . . help the grass grow.*

THE ECOSYSTEM JIGSAW

An ecosystem is like a jigsaw puzzle. It is made up of living things, such as plants and animals, and nonliving things, such as water and the Sun's energy.

All the pieces in the ecosystem jigsaw puzzle must fit together. If there's not enough rain on the African savanna, the grass withers and dies. Then the zebras that feed on the grass die, too. So do the lions that feed on the zebras.

All ecosystems, big and small, work in this way. A healthy ecosystem has many different species living in it. Each species helps keep the ecosystem working.

Zebras feed on the grass . . .   *. . . and provide food for lions.*

PESKY RABBITS

Humans often bring new plants and animals into an ecosystem. This can upset the delicate balance in that system. In 1859 in Australia, Thomas Austin released 24 rabbits onto his farm. With no foxes around to hunt them, the rabbit population exploded. There are now 200–300 million rabbits in Australia! They eat so many plants that many native animals find it difficult to survive.

Nature has its own way of keeping balance. If a community gets too big, it is often reduced by lack of food, predators, drought, disease, or fire (above).

A TEAM EFFORT

If one group of animals or plants disappears from an ecosystem, the entire ecosystem can break down. For example, sea otters might leave an area of the ocean. Then the sea urchins they feed on will multiply. The urchins will then eat so much kelp that the remaining kelp forest will die. With no kelp forest where sea otters can hide from sharks, killer whales, and other large predators, the sea otters will not return to the area.

In a well-balanced ocean ecosystem, sea otters and kelp help each other survive.

CHAPTER 10:
How Ecosystems Work

All living things need energy to grow, move around, and reproduce. Luckily, on Earth we have a constant source of energy—the Sun. Without it, life as we know it could not exist. Green plants use the Sun's energy to make their own food. This process is known as photosynthesis. Through photosynthesis, plants use energy from sunlight to convert water and carbon dioxide into food. This process also produces the oxygen that humans and animals need to breathe to stay alive.

THE ENERGY CHAIN

Animals can't produce their own food. Some animals get their energy from eating plants. Other animals get their energy by consuming plant eaters. But the energy chain doesn't stop there. Plants and animals release waste throughout their lives. This waste, which may be in the form of food or gases, returns energy back into the environment. And when plants and animals die, their remains rot, or decompose, and add nutrients to the soil.

Plants use sunlight to turn air and water into sugars. These sugars can then be used by the plants—and the animals that eat them—as food. This giraffe gets its energy from leaves high in the treetops.

HOW ECOSYSTEMS WORK

BIG BIOMASS

The combined weight of a species, or type of organism, is called its biomass. In the animal world, humans may seem to be the dominant species. But we make up less than 0.5 percent of all animal biomass. All the ants in the world probably weigh at least 20 times more than all the humans!

TOP OF THE PILE

An ecological pyramid illustrates how energy is passed on as it moves up the food chain of animals in an ecosystem. As energy flows through an ecosystem, some of it gets lost on the way. For example, animals lose heat from their bodies. Since there is less energy farther up the food chain, there are also fewer animals near the top of the chain.

A KILLER WHALE'S ECOLOGICAL PYRAMID

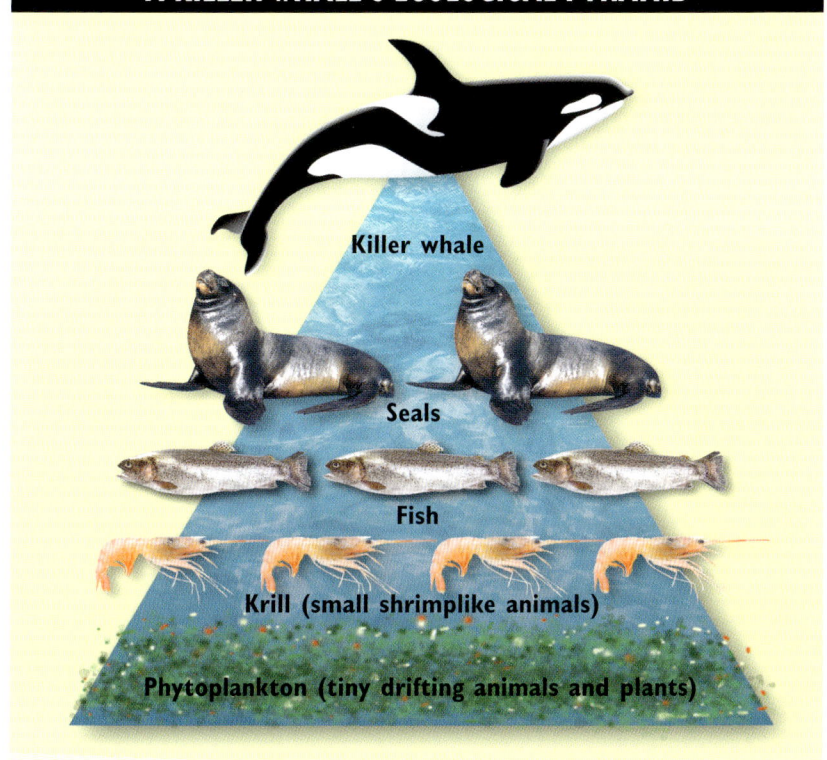

Killer whale
Seals
Fish
Krill (small shrimplike animals)
Phytoplankton (tiny drifting animals and plants)

Killer whales (orcas) are at the top of their food chain. They are much bigger than seals, fish, and other organisms lower down. In terms of biomass, however, the combined weight of all the organisms that the killers whales eat is greater than the weight of all the killer whales.

ENERGY FROM THE SUN TO YOUR TABLE

1) These corn plants use light from the Sun to turn air and water into sugars. The sugars can then be used by the plants as food. The energy in the sugars is passed on to the animals that eat the plants.

2) A field of corn uses energy from the Sun to produce the nourishment it needs to grow. When it is ripe, the corn is harvested and the ears of corn are separated from their stalks.

3) Corn that is grown for animals to eat is loaded into silos or other feeding bins. Ears of corn produced for humans to eat are displayed and sold in food markets.

4) A plateful of steaming-hot corn provides energy, flavor, and fun when prepared as nature provided it—right on the cob!

NATURAL CYCLES

Ecosystems are not just about animals eating one another and passing on energy. Plants and animals also need water, carbon, nitrogen, and other important elements to help them grow and repair their bodies. These elements are recycled again and again.

WATER

Water is a key part of life. You could survive for many weeks without food, but you would last only a few days without water. Water carries around nutrients inside all organisms. It also helps remove waste. That's why there is so much water in our bodies (and those of most animals). Around 70 percent of an adult human's body is made up of water. The water on our planet is constantly going through a huge recycling process called the water cycle (see page 39). The water cycle moves water from the oceans up into the atmosphere, down to the land, and back again.

Elephants must take in huge quantities of water to carry nutrients to every part of their large bodies. This is why they spend a great deal of time near water supplies.

A BIZARRE BIRTHDAY GIFT

Salmon give their young truly strange birthday presents—their own dead bodies! Soon after adult salmon spawn (lay their eggs), they die. Their rotting bodies add nutrients to the water. This is one way that young salmon get nourishment from the water. But some young go right to the source—the dead bodies of their parents!

THE CARBON CYCLE

Carbon is an element that is found in every living thing and many nonliving things, too. Plants absorb carbon dioxide from the atmosphere during photosynthesis. They then use the carbon to make carbohydrates. When animals eat plants, this carbon is passed on. Humans and animals give out carbon as carbon-dioxide gas. They release carbon into the atmosphere every time they breathe out.

Animals are living supplies of carbon. When they die, their rotting bodies return most of this carbon back to the atmosphere. All dead plants and animals contribute important nutrients and other substances to the soil when they die.

WONDERFUL WORLD

MINERAL CYCLES—THE NITROGEN CYCLE

Decomposing dung (manure) isn't everyone's favorite sight or smell. But it is part of another important cycle—the nitrogen cycle. Nitrogen is a gas. It makes up 78 percent of Earth's atmosphere. All living things need nitrogen to build proteins.

Plants and animals can't process nitrogen, but they can soak up nitrates in the ground—nitrates contain nitrogen. They are created by bacteria, lichens, and algae and help plants grow. When cows eat grass, they consume nitrates. And when they deposit dung, they also deposit nitrates. That is why the grass around rotting cow manure is often greener. Dung flies get in on the act, too. When these flies eat manure, they stir up small particles of the dung. This motion helps release the nitrates consumed by the animal.

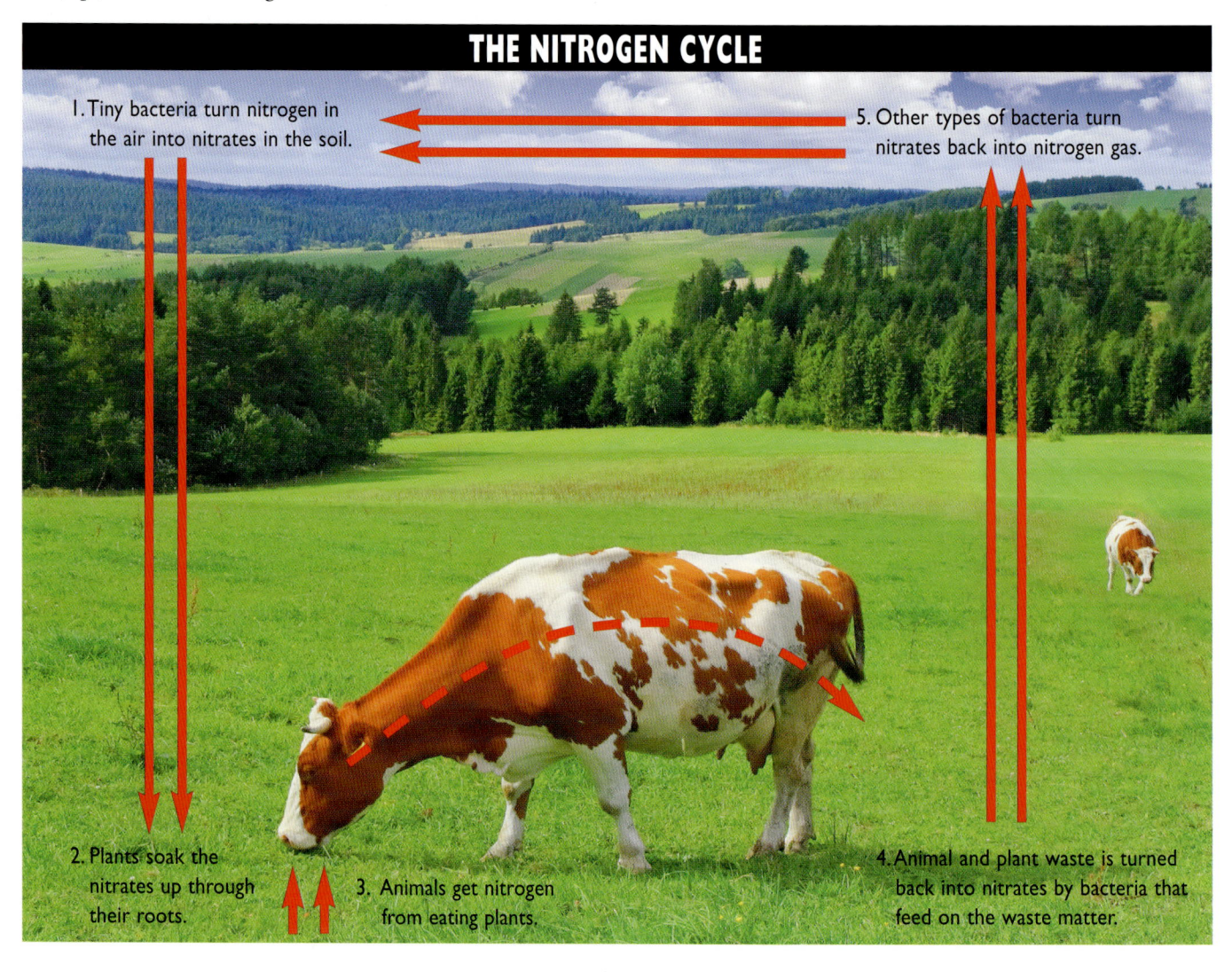

Without dung, our world would be a less pleasant place in which to live. We would have to use more artificial fertilizer on our crops, which would damage the environment.

THE NITROGEN CYCLE

1. Tiny bacteria turn nitrogen in the air into nitrates in the soil.
2. Plants soak the nitrates up through their roots.
3. Animals get nitrogen from eating plants.
4. Animal and plant waste is turned back into nitrates by bacteria that feed on the waste matter.
5. Other types of bacteria turn nitrates back into nitrogen gas.

HOW ECOSYSTEMS WORK

Too many human-made artificial nitrates in the soil can get into our drinking water and the atmosphere. Scientists suspect that taking in too many nitrates may cause diseases such as cancer and asthma.

TOO MUCH OF A GOOD THING

Farmers use nitrates as fertilizers to grow more crops. But the need for more nitrates has increased. Today we have developed ways of making artificial nitrates, but they can overload the natural system. As a result, they may hurt the ecological balance. Too many nitrates in rivers and lakes allow algae to grow in large numbers. The algae then use up oxygen in the water, killing fish and other wildlife.

OTHER MINERALS

Other important minerals are used by animals and plants. They include phosphorus, iron, sulfur, and calcium. Many of these minerals form in rocks deep underground. Most of them are then brought to the surface by volcanoes. On land, most animals get minerals from the water they drink. In the ocean, shellfish take calcium from the water and use it to make their shells.

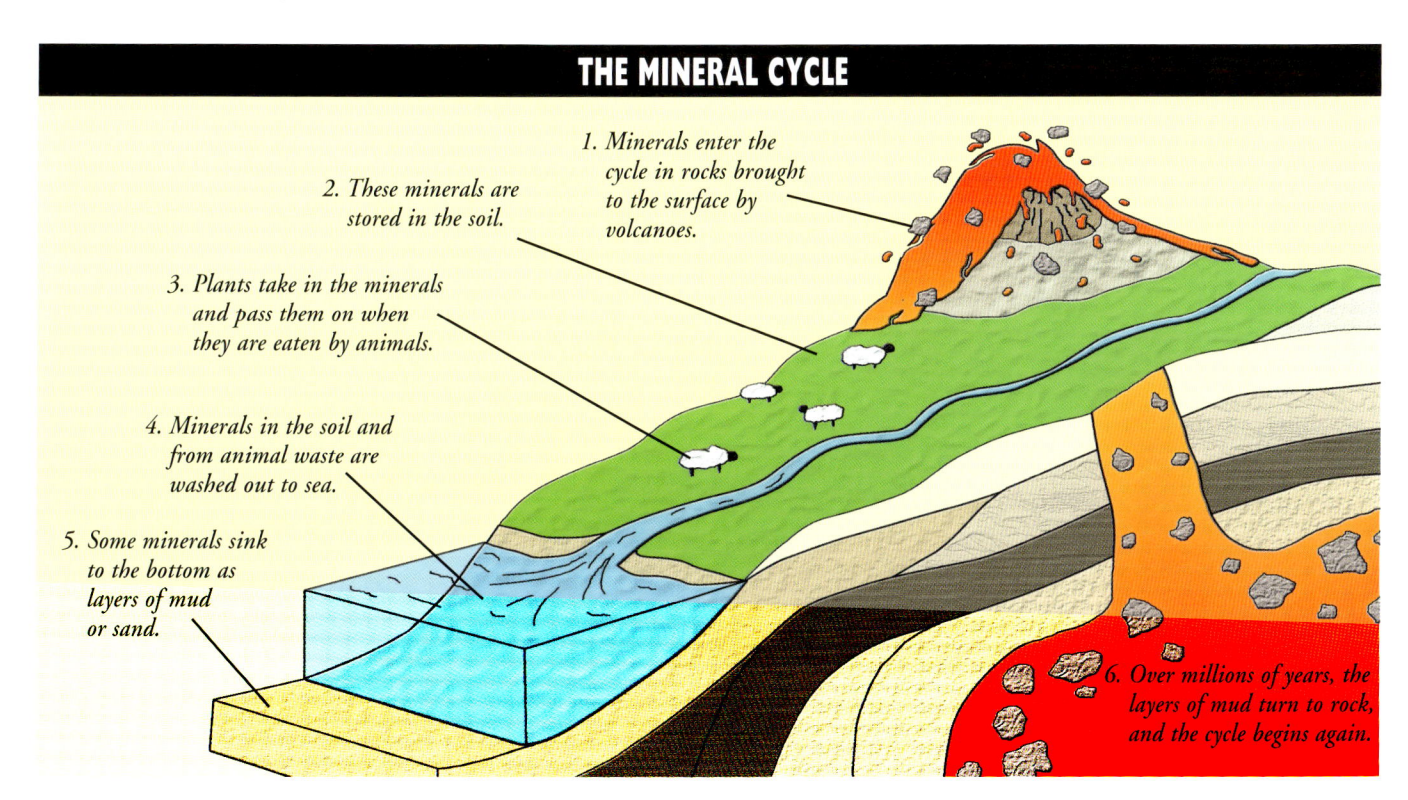

THE MINERAL CYCLE

1. Minerals enter the cycle in rocks brought to the surface by volcanoes.
2. These minerals are stored in the soil.
3. Plants take in the minerals and pass them on when they are eaten by animals.
4. Minerals in the soil and from animal waste are washed out to sea.
5. Some minerals sink to the bottom as layers of mud or sand.
6. Over millions of years, the layers of mud turn to rock, and the cycle begins again.

WONDERFUL WORLD

CHAPTER 11:
Living in an Ecosystem

The living things in an ecosystem are linked together by food chains. Food chains show who eats what—or whom!

Most often, at the bottom of the chain are plants, known as producers. They use the Sun's energy to make their own nutrients. These nutrients are passed on to plant-eating animals, known as primary consumers. They in turn are eaten by secondary consumers—meat eaters. At the top of the chain are big predators such as polar bears and sharks—tertiary consumers.

A food web combines food chains. These food chains interact with one another. Members of the same food web may compete with one another for food.

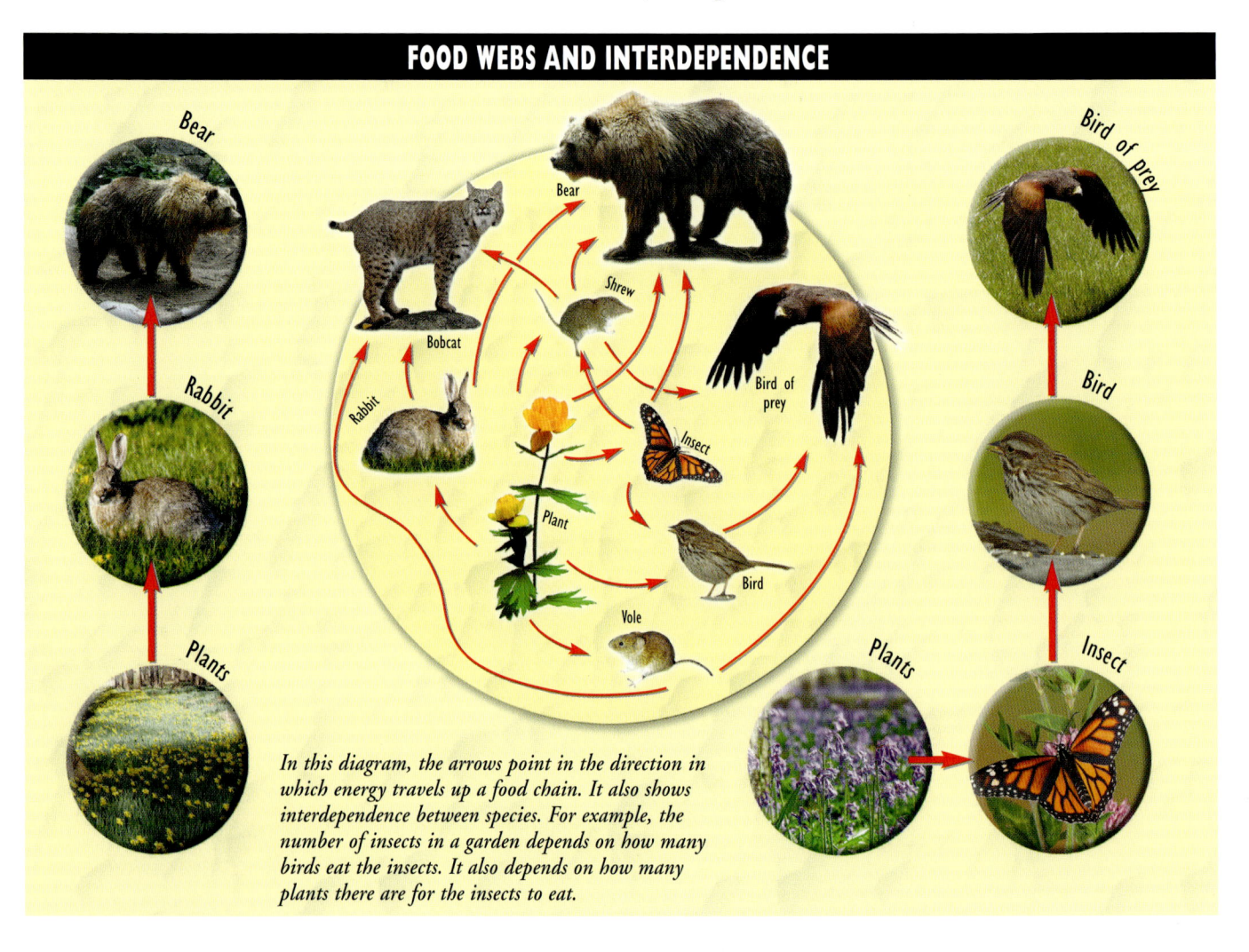

Sharks and other tertiary consumers get a lot of energy from eating meat. They need it. It's much harder work catching a seal than waiting for prey to simply drop by.

FOOD WEBS AND INTERDEPENDENCE

In this diagram, the arrows point in the direction in which energy travels up a food chain. It also shows interdependence between species. For example, the number of insects in a garden depends on how many birds eat the insects. It also depends on how many plants there are for the insects to eat.

LIVING IN AN ECOSYSTEM

IT'S A DIRTY JOB, BUT SOMEONE'S GOT TO DO IT!

An elephant munches away all day, but most of what it eats goes straight through it. So why is the ground not permanently covered with elephant droppings? Animals and plants known as decomposers feed off droppings. Decomposers break down the waste of other living things. Bacteria and fungi do most of the hard work. They are helped by maggots (usually fly larvae), dung beetles, and earthworms. Decomposers speed up the process of decomposition. In this way, they help put minerals back into the soil.

Two dung beetles roll a ball of manure. They will either eat it or lay their eggs inside it.

PREDATORS AND THEIR PREY

Every ecosystem has its share of interesting characters in its community of predators and prey.

CHEETAHS
Cheetahs can run at more than 60 mph (100km/h). However, the chase leaves them very worn out. They often have to rest for 20 minutes before they eat their kill.

A PREDATOR PLANT
The Venus flytrap has short, stiff trigger hairs on its leaves. When an insect touches a trigger hair, the leaf snaps shut and traps the insect. Inside, the plant has digestive juices to dissolve the insect's soft parts. After a few days, the leaf opens up again. The leftover hard pieces of the insect blow away.

SCAVENGER'S DELIGHT

Scavengers are animals such as flies, wasps, ravens, cockroaches, and even raccoons that eat dead animals and break them into small pieces. In this way, scavengers help start the process of decomposition. Vultures are among the best-known scavengers. This vulture (right) has picked the meat off the body of a dead cow.

DON'T GO NEAR THE WATER!

Piranhas live in rainforest rivers in South America. They change their behavior with the seasons. During the wet season, they are usually scavengers. But in the dry season, piranhas can turn into hunters. As the river-water levels go down, big groups of piranhas are forced to cluster in small patches of water. Together, they attack large animals that come to the river to drink. A piranha group can strip all the flesh off a large animal in just a few minutes.

WHAT MAKES A PERFECT HOME?

Animals living in an ecosystem are affected by the other animals and plants around them. But their environment also has a big impact on them. For desert plants and animals, finding and storing water is a much bigger problem than it is for animals that live in a rainforest. This is one reason that fewer plants and animals live in a desert than in a rainforest.

Almost all ecosystems depend on the Sun. The Sun provides energy for plants to make food. It also drives the water cycle by evaporating water into the atmosphere.

BIOTIC OR ABIOTIC

An ecosystem is affected by both living and nonliving factors. Soil, rocks, sunlight, and weather are all nonliving. They are known as abiotic factors. Animals and plants are living, or biotic, factors. Many animals and plants can survive only if the abiotic factors are just right. For example, the larvae (young) of spotted salamanders can survive only in water. Adult salamanders live on land. However, they must be near water in order to breed and lay their eggs.

Some animals have adapted to extreme abiotic factors. Teleost fish live in icy polar waters. Their bodies make a natural chemical that stops their blood from freezing.

ABIOTIC FACTORS

LIGHT AND HEAT
The Sun provides the energy plants need to make food. The Sun's energy also keeps animals warm.

LACK OF SUNLIGHT
In a shady wooded area, some grasses and other plants don't get enough sunlight for photosynthesis.

WATER
Without water, there would be no life.

LIVING IN AN ECOSYSTEM

Look at this picture of Monument Valley, Arizona. What abiotic factors can you see here? Compare the abiotic factors in this ecosystem with the abiotic factors where you live.

SOIL
Soil provides important nutrients that help plants grow. It also holds water for plants and animals to use.

ATMOSPHERE
The atmosphere is the giant blanket of air around Earth. It provides oxygen and carbon dioxide to ecosystems.

SHELTER
Cracks in a rock or an old wall provide shelter for snails, ants, wasps, and other tiny creatures.

SURVIVAL

Every ecosystem, whether it is big or small, is affected by abiotic factors. Many plants thrive in sunlight. Others do better in a cool, shady area beneath a tree. Plants have a better chance of surviving if they need different abiotic factors to live. This way, there are plenty of resources to go around.

Predators and abiotic factors ensure that no one plant or animal takes over. What if a small swarm of fruit flies had no predators and an endless supply of food? In less than one year there would be enough fruit flies to cover the entire planet! In nature, the numbers are kept down by the lack of food, many hungry predators, extreme weather, and disease.

POPULATIONS

All the animals in one species that live in an ecosystem are called a population. As populations get bigger or smaller, their effect on the rest of the ecosystem changes. All of the different populations in an ecosystem make up the community of that ecosystem.

Moss, like that growing on the side of this tree, survives when the abiotic factors in its environment include dampness and shade from sunlight.

LIVING IN AN ECOSYSTEM

NICHES

A niche describes the role that a plant or animal plays in its environment. An animal's niche tells us something about what it does, how it behaves, and the way it uses what is around it to survive. Niches also help animals and plants avoid competition for the same resources.

Unlike other species in their ecosystem, pandas feed almost entirely on bamboo. Feeding on a plant that almost no other animal eats helps pandas survive. This type of feeding creates a special niche for pandas in their ecosystem.

WINTER BREAK

Many animals' bodies have adapted over millions of years. These adaptations might help the animals find food, hide from predators, or survive in their habitat. During the winter, when food is scarce, bears go into a state resembling sleep. This is called hibernation. While a bear is hibernating, its body uses up less energy and it can live off its stored fat.

GETTING ALONG

Animals and plants living together in the same ecosystem make space for themselves in different ways.

SPREADING OUT

In a tropical rainforest, animals avoid competing with one another by living at different levels. Birds live in the treetops. Monkeys live on branches. Leopards and other larger animals spend most of their time on the forest floor.

KEEPING WATCH

Many animals, such as flocks of birds and herds of deer, live in groups. This allows them to watch out for danger while others are eating. Lions and wolves hunt in groups so that they can bring down buffalo, moose, and other large prey.

MARKING TERRITORY

Tigers are large hunters. They eat so much that they cannot afford to compete with other tigers in the same patch of forest. They urinate and leave scratch marks on trees to tell other tigers to stay away.

CHAPTER 12: Biomes

The world is divided into large regions called biomes. Every place on Earth is part of a biome. Most biomes support a wide variety of plant and animal life. Others, such as the polar regions of Antarctica and the Arctic, are so extreme that a limited number of species have adapted to life there.

Central American rainforests are perfect homes for the glasswing butterfly. It receives nutrients from the nectar found in the tropical plants that it visits.

The Arctic provides polar bears with plenty of seals and fish for their diet. When food is scarce, they may venture into towns to exploit another source of food—garbage!

BIOMES

LIFE ON LAND

Let's take a walking tour of some of Earth's biomes. We'll start at the equator and head north.

When you stand at the equator, you're probably in a rainforest biome. **Tropical rainforests** are hot and very rainy for most of the year. If you walk north, where it is still hot but rains less, you come across the subtropical forests of India and the dry **savanna** of East Africa. You might even find yourself in the subtropical wetlands of southern Florida known as the Everglades. Keep going!

Farther north, you come across hot, dry **deserts** in Africa, Asia, and North America. **Temperate grasslands** and **deciduous forests** await you in Europe, North America, and Asia. These biomes have warm summers and cold winters.

As you get closer to the North Pole, the trees are more likely to be conifers, part of the great northern **conifer forests** that stretch across Asia and North America. Finally you reach the cold deserts of the **tundra** and the icy **Arctic** regions of the far north.

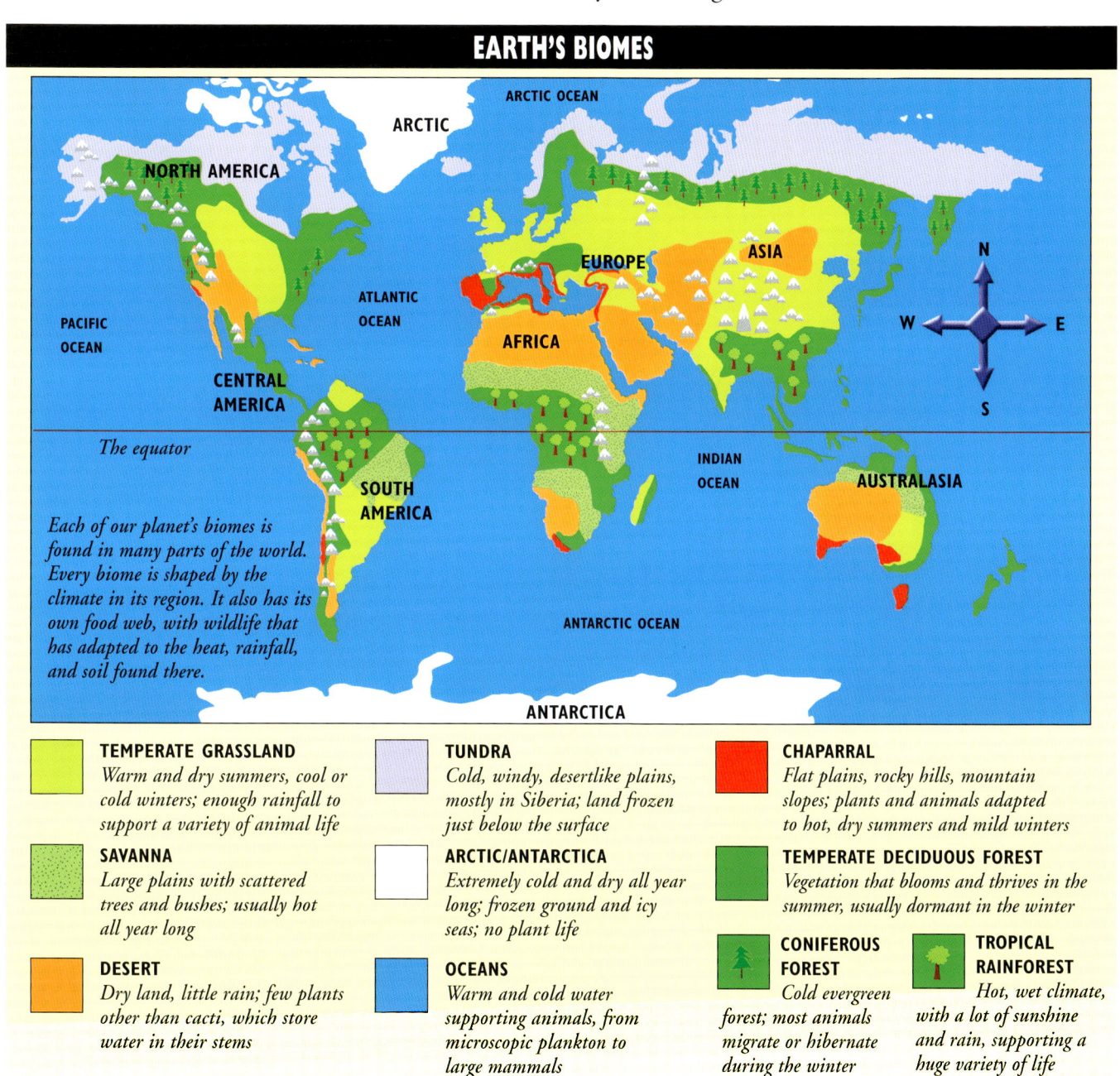

EARTH'S BIOMES

Each of our planet's biomes is found in many parts of the world. Every biome is shaped by the climate in its region. It also has its own food web, with wildlife that has adapted to the heat, rainfall, and soil found there.

TEMPERATE GRASSLAND
Warm and dry summers, cool or cold winters; enough rainfall to support a variety of animal life

SAVANNA
Large plains with scattered trees and bushes; usually hot all year long

DESERT
Dry land, little rain; few plants other than cacti, which store water in their stems

TUNDRA
Cold, windy, desertlike plains, mostly in Siberia; land frozen just below the surface

ARCTIC/ANTARCTICA
Extremely cold and dry all year long; frozen ground and icy seas; no plant life

OCEANS
Warm and cold water supporting animals, from microscopic plankton to large mammals

CHAPARRAL
Flat plains, rocky hills, mountain slopes; plants and animals adapted to hot, dry summers and mild winters

TEMPERATE DECIDUOUS FOREST
Vegetation that blooms and thrives in the summer, usually dormant in the winter

CONIFEROUS FOREST
Cold evergreen forest; most animals migrate or hibernate during the winter

TROPICAL RAINFOREST
Hot, wet climate, with a lot of sunshine and rain, supporting a huge variety of life

THE BLUE PLANET
Earth is often called the Blue Planet. This photograph from space shows why. Around 70 percent of Earth's surface is covered by water.

LIFE IN THE WATER
The oceans make up the largest biome on our planet. The food webs there contain everything from giant whales to microscopic phytoplankton.

The oceans need the Sun to give their animal and plant communities food and energy. Phytoplankton help with this process. Billions of phytoplankton float near the surface of the ocean. There they use light from the Sun to make food for themselves. Then they become food for bigger animals. Through the ocean food web, the Sun's energy is passed on up, even to fish-eating humans!

BIOMES

CORAL REEFS

With thousands of different species living together in a small area, coral reefs are complete ecosystems. Corals are groups of tiny animals with limestone shells. Within the coral animals are tiny single-celled algae. The algae use energy from the Sun to produce food for the corals. The corals then release nutrients to other types of algae. In this way, these members of the ecosystem help one another survive.

WATER ECOSYSTEMS

OCEANS

The ocean biome contains many ecosystems. In the deepest parts of Earth's oceans, ecosystems have developed where animals have adapted to life in the dark. The anglerfish swims around with a glowing fleshy "fishing rod" on its head. When the light attracts other fish, the anglerfish snaps them up quickly.

RIVERS

Five thousand species of fish live in the Amazon River in South America. One inhabitant of this river ecosystem is the electric eel. It can stun its prey with a 600-volt electric shock. Other members of the Amazon community are predators such as freshwater dolphins, otters, turtles, and giant anaconda snakes.

EXTREME BIOMES

There are ecosystems everywhere on Earth, even in the most extreme biomes. In Antarctica, for example, emperor penguins live with temperatures and wind that would freeze exposed human flesh in seconds.

At the other extreme is the baking heat of a sandy desert. In desert biomes, plants such as cacti can survive years of drought on water collected from a single rainfall. Animals such as kangaroo rats, snakes, and lizards are busy at night to avoid the daytime heat. During the day, they lie in burrows or under rocks.

Mountains are home to a wide range of plants and animals that can survive temperatures that go from baking to freezing in just a few hours. As you climb up a mountain, the climate, soil, and plant life change over very short distances.

LIFE AT INCREDIBLE DEPTHS

Almost 1 mi. (1.5km) beneath the ocean's surface, deep-sea vents gush out hot water loaded with minerals. Bacteria use the heat and minerals to make food. These bacteria and the food they produce are part of a food web that includes the tubeworm (below). The tubeworm exists on the food created by the bacteria. Tubeworms form protective tubes around themselves using their own secretions. The tubes can grow as long as 20 ft. (6m).

The cardon cactus lives in the Sonoran Desert, which is located in the United States and Mexico. It is the largest cactus in the world. The cardon's trunk can store almost one ton of water at one time. Its branches point upward, reducing the amount of its surface that faces the full effects of the hot sun.

SURVIVING EXTREME CONDITIONS

SPADEFOOT TOAD
The spadefoot toad lives in hot deserts in the southwestern U.S. It avoids the heat by hibernating underground for most of the year.

BACTRIAN CAMEL
The Gobi Desert in central Asia combines freezing cold winters with short, baking summers. The Bactrian camel can survive both. During the winter, it grows a thick coat and gets water from drinking snow. During the summer, it can go for months without water.

EMPEROR PENGUINS
Emperor penguins mate and lay eggs in the winter when Antarctic temperatures are as low as −40°F (−40°C). For more than two months, each father bird stands in freezing conditions incubating an egg on his feet. This enables the chick to hatch in the spring, giving it the best chance of survival.

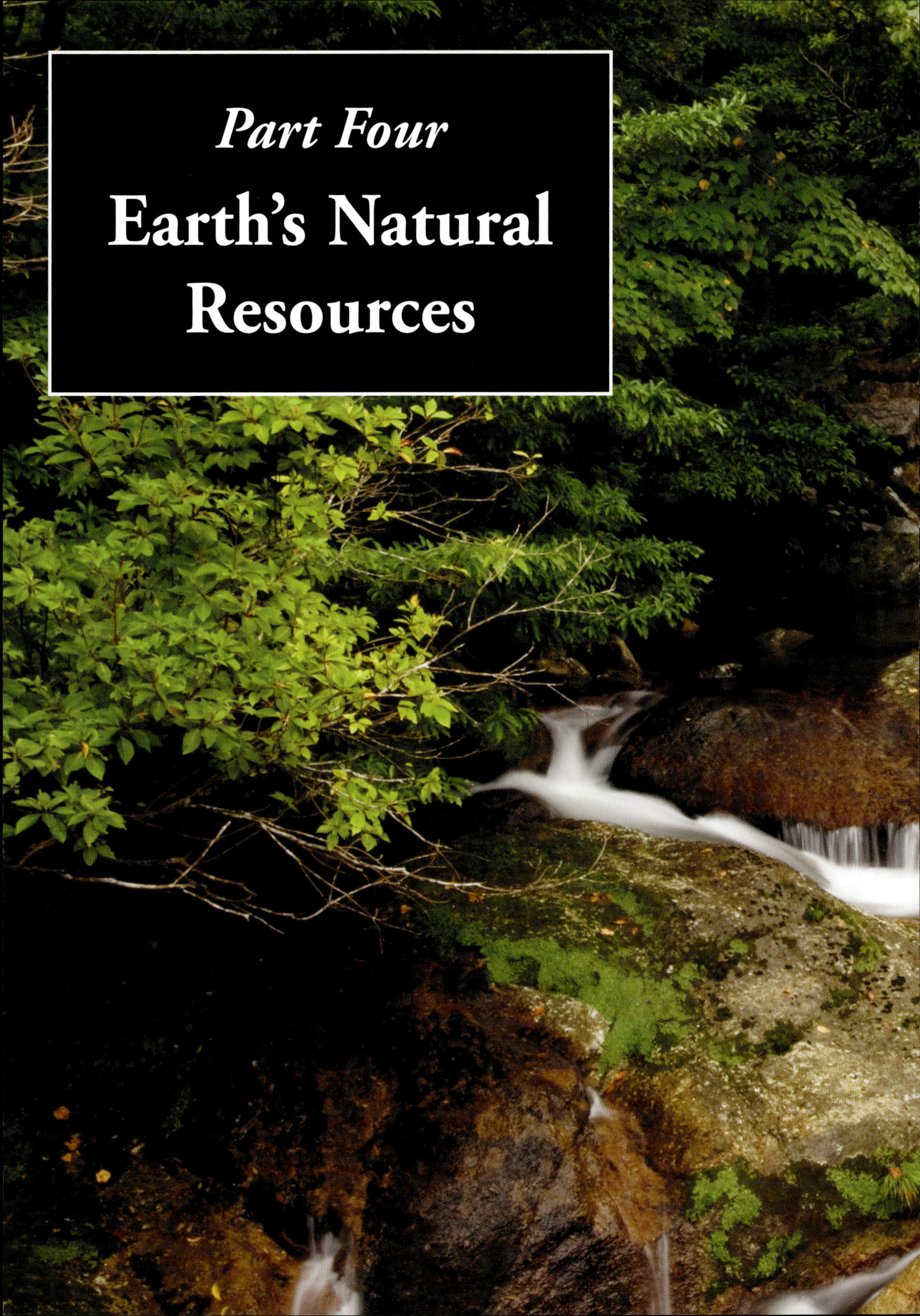

Part Four
Earth's Natural Resources

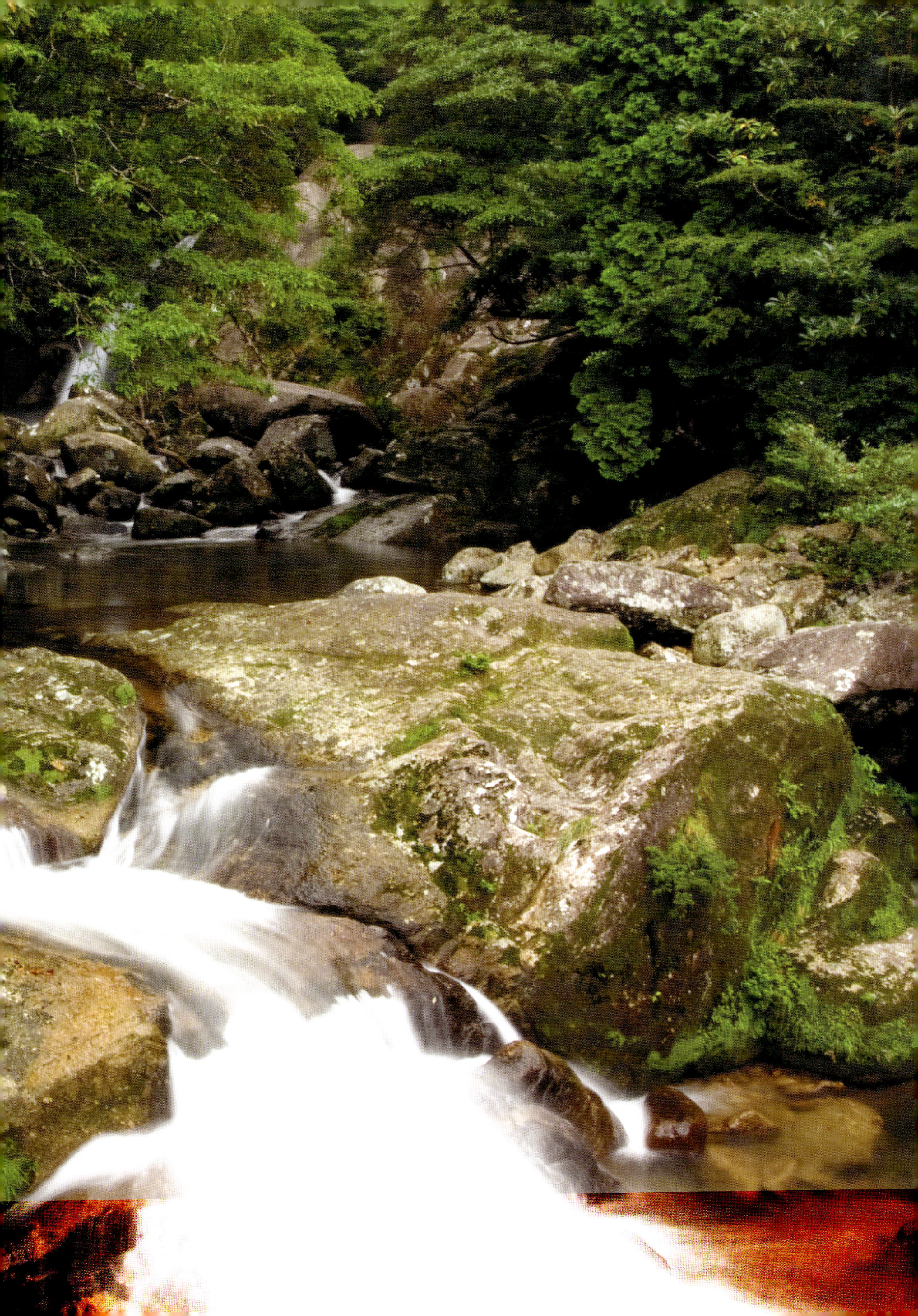

WONDERFUL WORLD

FRUIT
Fruit, like all plant resources, draws energy from the Sun.

FISH
Fish are among the many resources found in Earth's oceans.

WATER
People, animals, and plants need water to survive.

WIND POWER
Like water and sunlight, wind is a renewable resource and can be used to generate electricity.

CHAPTER 13: What Are Natural Resources?

Look around you. Everything in your daily life—your toothbrush, the food you eat, the clothes you're wearing, the heat in your home—can be traced back to Earth's natural resources. Natural resources are the materials and sources of energy that come from our planet.

GIFTS THAT KEEP ON GIVING

As their name tells us, Earth's resources come from nature. They include water, plant and animal life, coal, oil, minerals, and energy from wind and the Sun. People all over the world depend on Earth's natural resources

WATERY WORLD

Around 70 percent of Earth's surface is made up of water.

All the water on Earth today has been there since our planet was formed billions of years ago. And, as far as anyone knows, it is all the water that will ever be on Earth. Around 97 percent of Earth's water is salt water in the oceans. Less than three percent is fresh water. Most of Earth's fresh water is frozen in ice. It is in the glaciers of the Arctic and Antarctica and on mountains around the world. Water is considered a renewable resource. It is renewed through the water cycle (see page 39).

WHAT ARE NATURAL RESOURCES?

for their survival. We also depend on them to provide everything that helps make our lives more comfortable, interesting, and enjoyable. But it is up to us to take care of these resources. We need to be sure that they will be around for many generations.

Even a small area of land contains many natural resources. What resources do you see in this picture?

A WEALTH OF RESOURCES

SOIL
Rich soil is a resource that farmers work hard to protect. Many of today's farmers have learned natural ways to keep the soil healthy—while still getting good crops.

DIAMONDS
Diamonds are among the minerals called gemstones (see page 29). Like other minerals, they occur naturally. People value diamonds and other gems because they are so beautiful and difficult to find.

A NIGHT AT THE MOVIES
Everything these moviegoers are enjoying has its origins in natural resources. The fabric and metal in the seats come from cotton and iron ore. The popcorn comes from fields of corn. Even the film in the projector is made from petroleum!

DEFINING NATURAL RESOURCES

Natural resources may be grouped in several ways. One way is to list them as either renewable or nonrenewable. Renewable resources are those that nature can replace, recycle, or regrow in a short time. Animals, plants, water, solar energy, and wind energy are examples of renewable resources. But remember: some renewable resources can be used up if we waste them.

Fish from oceans, rivers, and lakes are renewable resources. However, overfishing is threatening the survival of some types of fish, such as the tuna that have been caught in this picture.

WHAT ARE NATURAL RESOURCES?

Most trees are said to be renewable. But replacing an old redwood tree—known as old growth—can take hundreds of years. So old-growth trees are nonrenewable.

Other resources are nonrenewable. This means that nature needs millions of years to create them. Examples of nonrenewable resources include oil, coal, natural gas, gold, silver, platinum, and other minerals. Today, people are using up these resources more quickly than nature can replenish them. When our supply of nonrenewable resources runs out, there won't be any more.

SOIL—WHAT TYPE OF RESOURCE IS IT?

Some natural resources are not easy to list as either renewable or nonrenewable. Soil is one example. Although many people consider soil nonrenewable, it can be renewed. But it takes many, many years. Nature may need thousands of years to make a few centimeters of healthy, mineral-rich soil.

LOSING RESOURCES

THE QUAGGA: EXTINCT
Thousands of quaggas once grazed on the plains of southern Africa, but they were hunted to extinction in the wild in around 1870. The last quagga in captivity died in a zoo in Amsterdam, Netherlands, in 1883.

HAWAIIAN BIRDS: THREATENED
The mongoose was brought to Hawaii in 1883 to help control the islands' rat population. However, mongooses began eating bird eggs, which caused a threat to Hawaii's ground-nesting birds.

THE ARAL SEA: THREATENED
The Aral Sea sits on the border between Khazakstan and Uzbekistan. Over the last 30 years, this sea has lost 60 percent of its water volume. Since the 1960s, its water sources have been used for irrigation. These satellite images show the sea in August 1989 (left) and August 2003.

Iron ore is an inorganic resource. Here it is heated to create steel in a process called smelting. The large hot orange steel sheet is being rolled by a machine in a steel mill.

ORGANIC AND INORGANIC RESOURCES

Natural resources can also be grouped as either organic or inorganic. Organic resources come from things that are or were once alive. Inorganic resources do not come from living organisms.

INORGANIC RESOURCES

Minerals and rocks are examples of inorganic materials. Our daily lives are filled with examples of these resources. The soda can you recycled today is made from aluminum. Your mother's earrings have opals in them. The construction-site crew down the block is using steel in the buildings that are being put up.

SKYSCRAPING RESOURCES

The Sears Tower in Chicago, Illinois, is North America's tallest building. It stands 1,500 ft. (442m) and 110 stories tall. It was built with 68,946 tons of steel, which is made from the natural resource of iron ore.

WHAT ARE NATURAL RESOURCES?

These tiny tree seedlings will eventually be planted as forests. The trees will grow and then be cut down for timber.

This forest of trees has been grown as a crop that will be harvested for wood.

ORGANIC RESOURCES

Organic resources include plants and animals. Think about all the ways you use organic resources in a single day. You might wear clothes made out of cotton or lamb's wool. Lunch might be a cheese sandwich and an apple. Your schoolwork is written on paper, maybe at a desk—both of which are made out of wood.

As a renewable organic resource, trees are often grown to be harvested, just like many other plants. Whole forests are grown to be cut down for the wood they produce. The careful cultivation of new crops of trees ensures that these resources stay renewable.

WOOL—AN ORGANIC RESOURCE

Wool is only one product that sheep give us. We also eat their meat (as lamb and mutton) and make cheeses (such as feta) and yogurt from their milk.

A sheep produces a fleece.

The sheep is sheared.

The fleece is spun into wool.

Wool is made into clothes and other textiles.

WONDERFUL WORLD

Natural gas forms alongside oil. Early oil drillers considered it worthless. They burned it just to get rid of it! Some countries do this even today.

CHAPTER 14: Nonrenewable Resources

Nonrenewable resources are found on Earth in limited amounts. This means that they cannot be replaced easily. At least, that is, they cannot be replaced as quickly as many of them are being used. And people have been using some of them faster and faster.

FOSSIL FUELS

Many nonrenewable resources are fossil fuels. Among them are oil, natural gas, and coal. Fossil fuels have been forming in Earth's crust (the outermost solid layer of the planet) for millions of years. They are called fossil fuels because they are made from the decaying remains of animals, plants, and other organisms.

These rigs (right) drill for oil around the clock. We use this oil in our cars and to heat our homes. The oil was formed from organisms that lived in water millions of years ago. Oil deposits found today might once have been covered by oceans or seas.

NONRENEWABLE RESOURCES

Some of this decaying plant and animal matter fell to the ocean floor and was covered over by sediment. Some of the matter was buried deep under the ground. In both cases, the organic matter was covered over by layer after layer of other materials. It all became part of Earth's crust. There it sat for millions of years, compressed beneath the heat and weight of the rock covering it. Slowly the material formed fossil fuels.

DRILLING FOR OIL

The first oil well was drilled in Titusville, Pennsylvania, 1859. There, a retired railroad conductor named Edwin Drake struck oil on his farm. People were first interested in oil for use in kerosene lamps. Its use in cars and heating came later. But Drake's discovery still started the modern oil industry. His well was the first drilled solely for the purpose of finding oil.

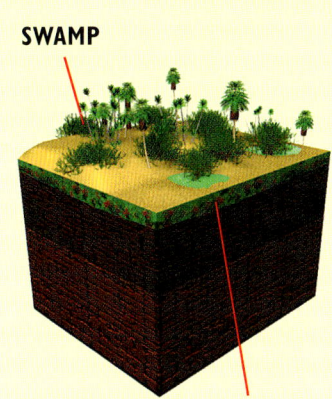

HOW COAL FORMED

SWAMP
PLANT DEBRIS

Around 300 million years ago, tree-filled swamps covered most of Earth. As plants and trees died, they settled to the bottom of these swamps. There, this matter began to decay.

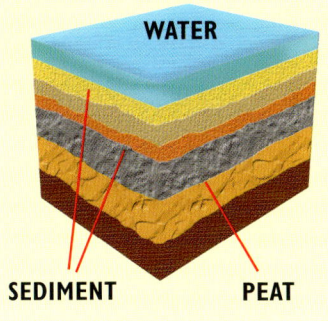

WATER
SEDIMENT **PEAT**

The decaying matter formed peat. This spongy material was soon buried under more layers.

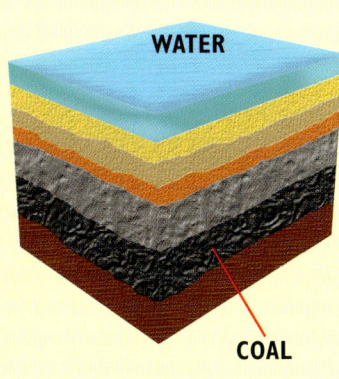

WATER
COAL

After millions of years of pressure and heat, the peat became coal.

USING FOSSIL FUELS

Roughly 80 percent of the energy used worldwide comes from fossil fuels. Most of these fossil fuels, such as oil, natural gas, and coal, must be changed, or converted, in some way to create energy that we can reuse. Today, through technology, we are able to convert fossil fuels to usable energy more and more efficiently.

Oil and natural gas are very much in demand as energy sources today. And no wonder! They power our vehicles. They heat our homes and businesses. They are also used to make plastics, medicines, cosmetics, synthetic fabrics, and many other products.

Oil is used to make some surprising items—such as ink for printing money, asphalt for roads, lipstick, and even sneakers.

NONRENEWABLE RESOURCES

A LOOK AT HOW FOSSIL FUELS ARE USED

FOSSIL FUEL	MAJOR PRODUCERS	USE OF FOSSIL FUEL
Oil	Saudi Arabia, Russia, United States	• As gasoline, diesel fuel, and jet fuel to power cars, buses, trains, and airplanes • Heat • Manufacturing plastics, synthetic clothing (such as nylon, polyester, Kevlar), cosmetics, medicines, fertilizers, insecticides, etc.
Coal	China, United States, India	• Fuel for heat, light, and generating electricity
Natural gas	United States, Russia, Canada	• Fuel for light, heat, cooking, manufacturing, and generating electricity

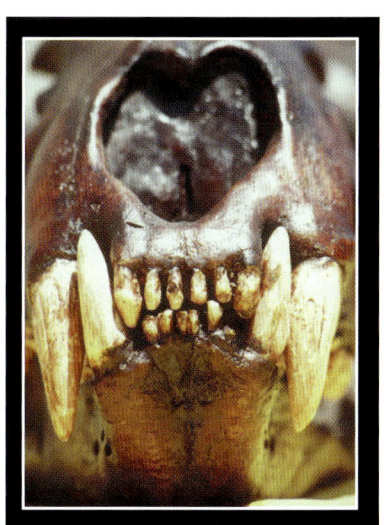

LA BREA: TREASURE TROVE OF DEATH

Tar pits form when crude oil from Earth's crust seeps up to the surface through cracks. The La Brea Tar Pits in Los Angeles, California, are famous for their collection of fossilized animals and plants from the Pleistocene period. The remains of insects, reptiles, amphibians, birds, fish, and even mammals, such as saber-toothed tigers (above), have been discovered.

THE POLITICS OF OIL

Today, uses for oil continue to rise. Quantities of it, however, continue to decrease.

Many nations have large supplies of oil beneath their land. Others need that oil for their own use. One third of the largest oil-supplying nations are in the Middle East. The nations that use the most oil are China, Japan, and the industrialized nations of Europe and North America. These factors affect the balance between the world's oil supply and the demand for oil. They also affect the economies and politics of the West and the Middle East.

This container ship is powered by diesel or another oil-based fuel. Most of its cargo consists of oil-based products, and the containers holding the cargo are made of oil-based materials. The hold of this ship is also probably carrying oil, which will power other means of transportation.

In large urban settings such as Los Angeles, Califorinia (right), burning fossil fuels causes air pollution. Exhaust fumes from cars, trucks, and other vehicles are a major contributor.

PROBLEMS WITH FOSSIL-FUEL RESERVES

Humans have found many uses for coal, natural gas, and oil. But using these fossil fuels also has its problems. The biggest is pollution. Most fossil fuels must be burned to be used. Burning them releases their energy. Only then do they create heat, produce electricity, or otherwise perform as we need them to. As they burn, however, they also release the following harmful substances into the atmosphere:

- **Carbon monoxide:** This adds to urban smog, air pollution, and global warming.

- **Sulfur dioxide:** This comes from coal and causes acid rain.

- **Particulates:** These tiny pieces of matter are released by burning fuel and are not healthy for people to breathe.

MAJOR AIR POLLUTANTS AND THEIR SOURCES

These two charts show some of Earth's major air pollutants (below left) and the sources of these pollutants (below right). The percentage of pollutants in the atmosphere as a whole may be a tiny fraction of one percent. But this tiny amount can still be very harmful.

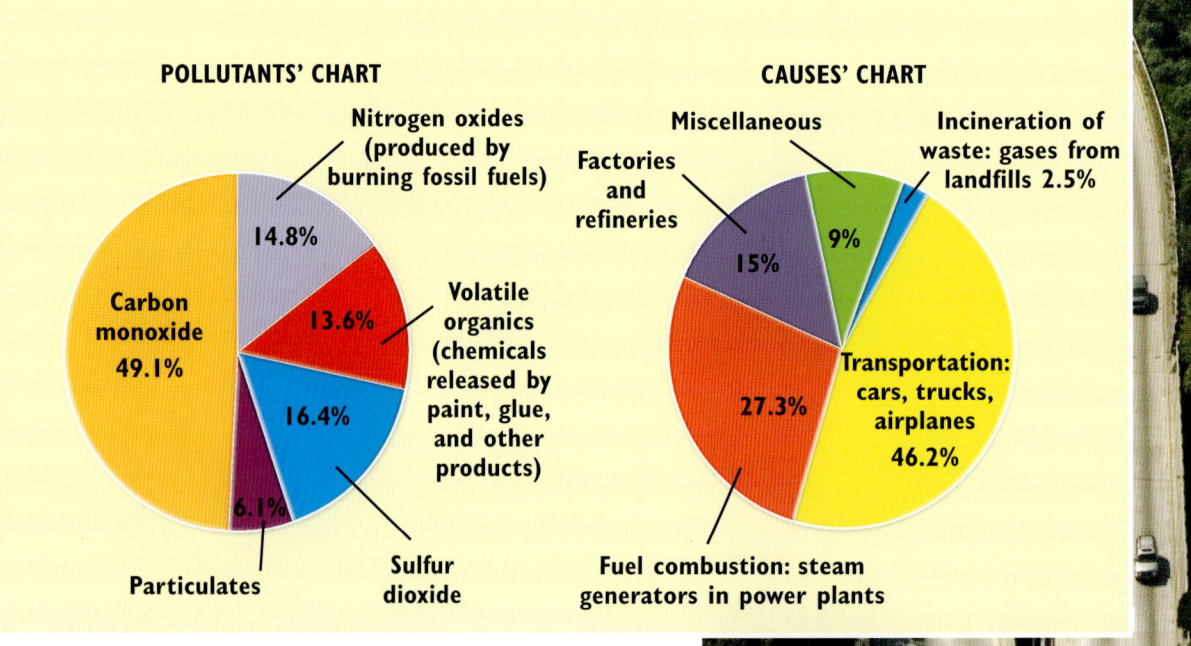

POLLUTANTS' CHART

- Carbon monoxide 49.1%
- Nitrogen oxides (produced by burning fossil fuels) 14.8%
- Volatile organics (chemicals released by paint, glue, and other products) 13.6%
- Sulfur dioxide 16.4%
- Particulates 6.1%

CAUSES' CHART

- Transportation: cars, trucks, airplanes 46.2%
- Fuel combustion: steam generators in power plants 27.3%
- Factories and refineries 15%
- Miscellaneous 9%
- Incineration of waste: gases from landfills 2.5%

NONRENEWABLE RESOURCES

A RISKY BUSINESS

Aside from the pollution, getting to these fossil fuels is difficult. They are often buried deep in the ground—right where they formed. They must be brought to the surface by mining, drilling, piping, or other means. These methods can be harmful to both the planet and the people who collect them.

Underground mines put miners in danger of mine collapse and lung disease from breathing coal dust. But strip-mining (above) can scar the land as the topsoil is stripped away to get at the coal beneath.

OIL SPILLS

Oil spills are a danger whenever crude oil must be transported. Spills can kill animals and destroy entire ecosystems. They can also harm communities and industries along coasts. In 1979, the tanker *Atlantic Empress* collided with the tanker *Aegean Captain*. The two ships spilled 276,000 tons of oil into the Caribbean Sea. This is the worst oil tanker spill on record.

WONDERFUL WORLD

DANGEROUS DIAMONDS
Many diamonds come from Africa. But Russia, Canada, Australia, and Brazil are also big suppliers of diamonds. Mining diamonds can be brutal, dangerous work. Once mined, diamonds have many uses. As rare and precious minerals they are cut and polished to become expensive jewelry. As the hardest minerals known diamonds are used in industry for grinding, polishing, and cutting machine parts and other hard substances—including other diamonds!

MINERAL AND ROCK RESOURCES
Minerals and rocks are also nonrenewable resources. They make up Earth's crust and other solid parts of our planet.

A HUGE AND VARIED RESOURCE
Scientists have identified 3,800 different minerals. Some, such as ores, contain metals. The metals can be stripped out and used in construction and manufacturing. They are especially useful in electrical supplies. Metals are good conductors of heat and electricity. Other rare minerals, like rubies and emeralds, are often used in jewelry. Precious metals like gold, silver, and platinum may also be used in jewelry.

Quartz is one of the world's most commonly found mineral resources.

NONRENEWABLE RESOURCES

Like any other mineral, salt must be taken from Earth. Here, workers gather halite (the scientific name for salt) from the Colchani Salt Pans in Bolivia. The salt pans are large plains made entirely of the salt that will eventually be used to season our food.

A STABLE AND RELIABLE RESOURCE

The term *mineral* is often used for anything nonliving taken from the ground. But it actually refers to specific substances. True minerals have set chemical makeups. A mineral will be the same no matter where it is found. This is not true of rocks. Samples of the same type of rock may have very different chemical makeups.

THE PROPERTIES OF MINERALS: A SHORT GLOSSARY

Some common properties of minerals include the following:

Color: a mineral's true color.

Cleavage: the way a mineral breaks along its planes in parallel lines, creating a smooth surface. Mica is known for this.

Crystal form: the arrangement of a mineral's atoms. Amethyst's crystals form in angular shapes on its surface.

Fracture: the way a mineral separates if it does not break along its planes.

Hardness: this is measured on a scale devised by German geologist Friedrich Mohs.

Luster: the way a mineral reflects light.

Specific gravity: a mineral's weight compared to an equal volume of water.

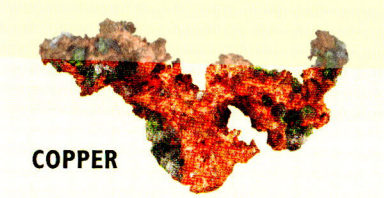

COPPER

MICA

AMETHYST

METALS: A USEFUL RESOURCE

Metals are often extracted from other resources such as minerals. Once mined, a metal can be combined with other substances to produce an alloy.

NICKEL
Nickel is used mostly as an alloy. Combined with iron, it gives great strength to steel. The nickel used in coins is actually an alloy made up mostly of copper.

TUNGSTEN
Tungsten melts at 6,170°F (3,410°C), making it the most heat-resistant metal known. It is used as the wire filament in light bulbs.

ALUMINUM
Aluminum is lightweight yet strong. It can be shaped easily when heated and stays tough under extreme cold. Aluminum is one of the most useful metals known. It is used for tinfoil, cans, and in building materials.

CHAPTER 15: Renewable Resources

Earth's renewable resources are those that can be replaced in a short amount of time. Energy from the Sun, water, wind, animals, and plants are all renewable resources.

SMART AND NECESSARY

Even the air we breathe and the heat produced inside Earth are resources. Water, sunlight, and plants are crucial to life on the planet. So taking care of Earth's renewable resources isn't just smart—it is necessary.

ECOSYSTEMS: RENEWABLE RESOURCES AT WORK

An ecosystem is a community in nature. It is any place where plants and animals depend on one another for survival (see Chapter 9). Within each ecosystem the animals and plants are renewable resources. They also depend on other renewable resources, such as water and the Sun, to exist in their ecosystem.

Water. Air. Wind. Sun. We live every day with a number of renewable resources at our fingertips. Earth has more renewable than nonrenewable resources.

RENEWABLE RESOURCES

In a garden, plants rely on the soil and atmosphere for water and carbon dioxide. They also use energy from sunlight to convert the carbon dioxide and water into food (carbohydrates). Plants are a resource to honeybees, birds, and other animals that eat them or drink their nectar. In turn, these animals carry pollen from one plant to another. This helps the plants reproduce.

Plant-eating animals are a resource to meat-eating animals. When plant eaters are eaten, the nutrients produced by the plants enter the meat eaters' bodies.

When plants, insects, and other organisms die, their decaying remains become a resource that adds nutrients to the soil. This provides nourishment to worms and insects.

HELPING ECOSYSTEMS HELP THEMSELVES

By monitoring the condition of Earth's ecosystems, we can help nature maintain a balance among the many renewable resources that keep an ecosystem healthy.

CUTTING DOWN WITH CARE
Forests can stay renewable as long as people help them replenish their own supply of trees. Planned and controlled logging keeps forests free of sick and dying trees.

MANAGING ANIMAL NUMBERS
Control of animal populations assures food for all. Too many fish in one place can deplete their food supply. Overfishing can deprive water resources of their balance between plant and animal life.

WATER FOR ALL
Dams control the flow of water and create lakes and reservoirs. They can provide a source of drinking water and habitats for wildlife. However, they can also sometimes harm habitats.

WIND POWER

Wind power is created by harnessing the power of the wind. In the past, people used windmills. Today they use powerful wind turbines. Both capture the energy from the wind, using it to turn the blades at the top of a tower. A wind turbine's turning blades are used to generate electricity.

ALTERNATE ENERGY SOURCES

Solar energy. Wind energy. Hydroelectric power. Geothermal power. Tidal power. Alternate energy sources offer some exciting possibilities both for now and into the future.

Some of these energy sources—like solar, wind, and hydroelectric power—have been tested. All of them have found some use and success. But for all of these sources, even if taken together as a group, their use is still small compared to our total energy consumption.

Wind power is renewable, and it doesn't pollute. But some people think a hillside dotted with giant wind turbines, as seen here in the Mojave Desert in the United States, is an eyesore and makes too much noise.

RENEWABLE RESOURCES

Heated water from the Svartsengi geothermal power plant in Grindavik, Iceland, flows to a famous health spa called the Blue Lagoon.

GEOTHERMAL POWER

Geothermal power comes from using the heat of Earth itself. This heat, in the form of hot water and steam, is often found in areas of volcanic activity. With pipes and pumps, the water or steam is taken from underground reservoirs. It is used to power turbines that then generate electricity.

TIDAL POWER

Like hydroelectric power, tidal power also uses energy from water. In this case, the energy is generated by the tides that advance and recede in oceans and large lakes. Dams stretching over bays capture water at high tide. Later, as water is released with the outgoing tide, the movement powers turbines and generates electricity.

ALTERNATE ENERGIES AT WORK

SOLAR POWER
Solar power comes from the Sun. Energy from the Sun is collected by capturing its rays in special solar panels. This energy is converted to electricity, which then becomes an energy source for running all of a building's appliances, including sources for heating and cooling. In the picture above, a parking meter is powered by a solar panel.

HYDROELECTRIC POWER
Hydroelectric power is generated by moving water. Power plants built over flowing rivers convert the water's energy into electrical energy. First the water is stored behind a dam. As the water is released, the movement turns huge turbine blades. This in turn generates electricity.

THE OXYGEN CYCLE

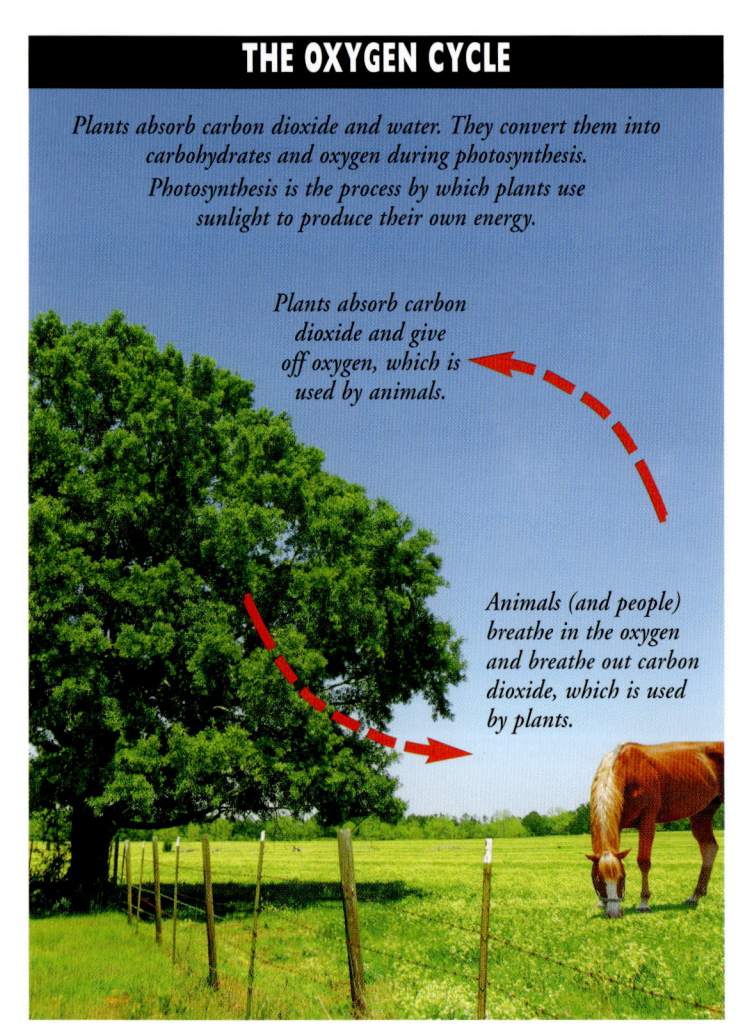

Plants absorb carbon dioxide and water. They convert them into carbohydrates and oxygen during photosynthesis. Photosynthesis is the process by which plants use sunlight to produce their own energy.

Plants absorb carbon dioxide and give off oxygen, which is used by animals.

Animals (and people) breathe in the oxygen and breathe out carbon dioxide, which is used by plants.

PLANT RESOURCES

It would be easy to overlook plants as valuable natural resources. As part of the oxygen cycle, plants play a key role in renewing the oxygen in Earth's atmosphere. Without plants, humans and animals would not have oxygen to breathe.

Plants are also a food resource in all of Earth's ecosystems. For humans in particular, plants are a food source, whether growing wild or as crops that we plant and harvest.

RAINFOREST TREASURES

Many scientists think that around two thirds of all plant species in the world are found in rainforests. These plants produce as much as 40 percent of Earth's oxygen. Rainforest plants have given us hundreds of varieties of fruit, vegetables, and spices. The raw materials for many products, from rubber to chewing gum, come from rainforest trees.

MEDICINE CABINET TO THE WORLD

Scientists estimate that plants from the rainforest have provided the basis for around 25 percent of the world's medicines. From compounds that help heal wounds to drugs that fight cancer, especially leukemia and other childhood cancers, Earth's rainforests could hold the promise for future success in treating illness and disease.

Warm, wet rainforests—like this one in Madagascar—have more types of trees than anywhere else on Earth. Protecting rainforests also means protecting countless plant and animal species.

RENEWABLE RESOURCES

PAPER OR FORESTS?

It's no secret that Earth's rainforests are in danger. It has been estimated that around 122 sq. mi. (315km^2) of rainforest is cut down every year for logging and to create farmland. Most of the logging industry is based on the demand for wood and paper products.

Around 95 percent of all paper is made from wood, but now paper can be efficiently and successfully reused through recycling. Think of how many trees could be saved just from recycling the daily newspaper! If you can't find recycled paper, try to buy paper from forests where trees are replanted (see page 85).

ANIMAL RESOURCES

Just like plants, animals are a renewable resource. In viewing animals as a resource, you might first think of them as sources of food or other products for people. Fish, for example, feed people all over the world. Sheep, goats, and cattle give milk and meat. Hides from many animals have value when building shelters or as clothing and shoes.

Animals also have a major effect on the environment. Each animal helps balance the ecosystem of which it is a part. Fish feed people. They also feed sharks in the ocean. Coyotes have been known to kill sheep and sometimes

Some animals, such as cattle, are such important resources that humans have domesticated, or tamed, them. Herds of cattle are raised all over the world.

ANIMALS AT WORK

PACK ANIMALS
Some animals have many uses. Llamas, like camels, horses, and even elephants, are called pack animals. This means they are used to carry things. Llamas also have hair that makes a useful fiber.

AQUACULTURE
Some fish, such as salmon and trout, are both caught in the wild and farmed. Fish-farming is known as aquaculture. As world supplies in the wild have declined, fish-farming has grown. According to recent figures, 43 percent of all fish eaten comes from farms.

WHOSE RESOURCE?
The North American northern spotted owl prefers nesting in old-growth forests. Old-growth forests have a lot of undergrowth and decaying trees. The owl has become the focus of a debate between environmental groups and companies that log these forests for their ancient and highly valuable trees.

get into garbage in urban areas. But they also control the rodent population around farms and towns. Each of these animals plays an important role in its own ecosystem.

THE BIG PICTURE
Each individual ecosystem contributes to the health of our planet, which is a collection of ecosystems. Sometimes, however, humans exploit the resources in one ecosystem. We cut down too many trees in a rainforest or damage the landscape while mining for coal. We have to think about the effect this might have on the planet as a whole.

THE AMERICAN BISON
In the 1800s, bison populations on the Great Plains of North America may have been as large as 75 million. Native Americans relied on the bison for food, clothing, and fuel. Nonnative settlers hunted it aggressively—often just for sport. They almost drove it to extinction. By the 1880s, the bison population may have been as low as 1,000. The government and conservationists worked to protect the bison, and its population has grown again. But it will never reach the huge numbers it once had.

Part Five
Caring for Planet Earth

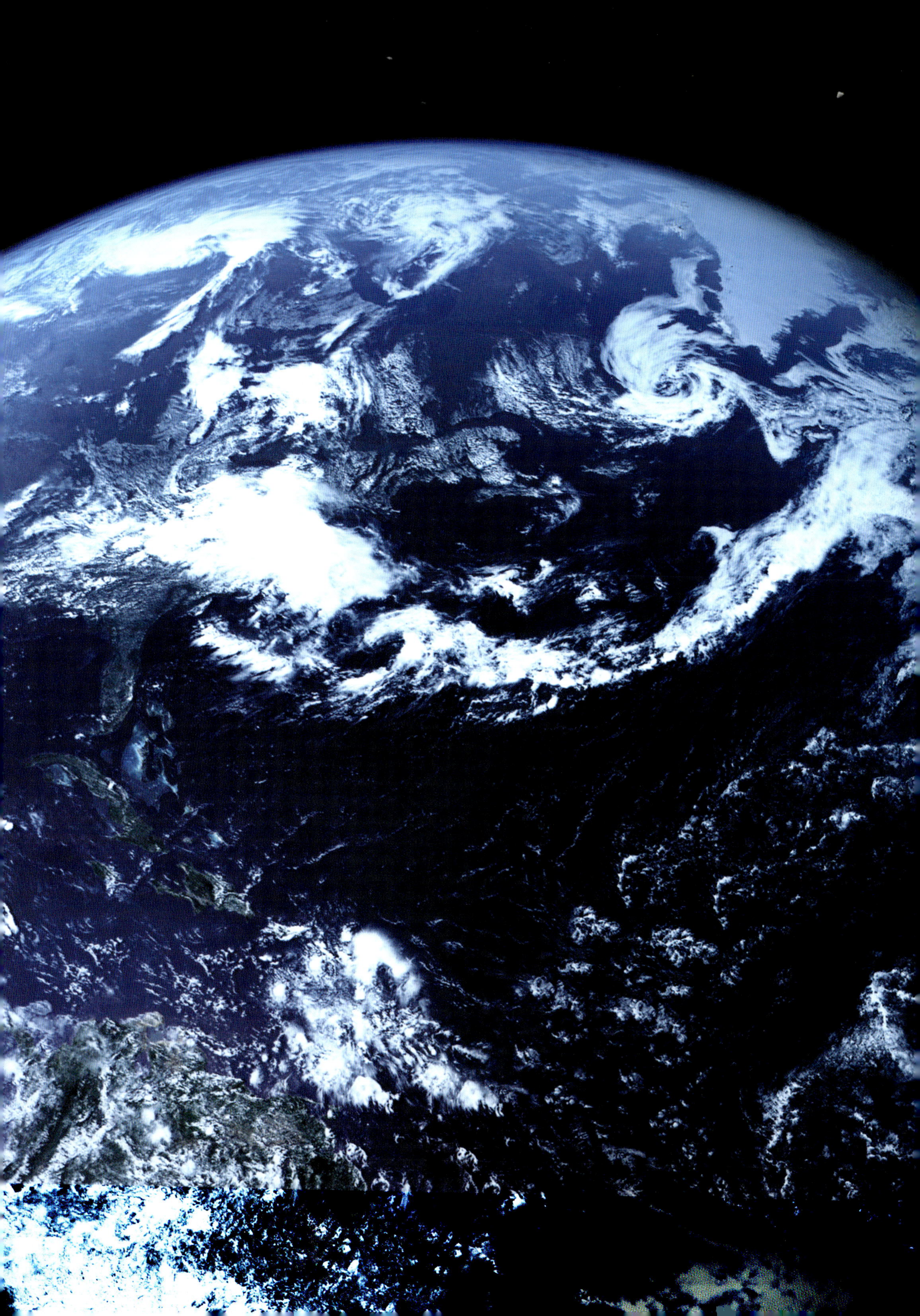

CHAPTER 16: Climate Change

Hold onto your seat—it's going to be a bumpy ride! The future looks set to get stormier as the world's climate warms up. Earth's climate has become hotter and colder throughout history, but scientists now believe it is heating up faster than ever before.

GOOD GASES

Temperatures on Mars average around –76°F (–60°C). Without our greenhouse gases, Earth's climate would be similar. We need some greenhouse gases to survive—but too much of them could be very dangerous.

HOW DO WE KNOW?

Layers of ice dating back hundreds of thousands of years are frozen on Antarctica. Gases and chemicals trapped in the ice can give scientists important information about how greenhouse gases have affected Earth in the past. Scientists collect "cores" of ice that can be studied like icy timelines of Earth's climate.

CLIMATE CHANGE

GREENHOUSE GASES
Gases such as carbon dioxide, methane, and water vapor do an important job. They trap heat from the Sun and keep our planet warm enough for life. However, for the past 200 years, people have been using more and more energy. Fossil-fuel-burning cars and power plants create huge amounts of carbon dioxide. This traps more and more heat from the Sun.

GLOBAL WARMING
Scientists don't know exactly how much warmer Earth will get—possibly 5°F (2°C) by 2050. This doesn't sound like much, but it could turn many parts of the world into deserts, causing food and water shortages. If the polar icecaps start melting on a large scale, sea levels will rise. This will create a serious risk of flooding for many coastal towns and cities.

EFFECTS OF GLOBAL WARMING

RISING SEA LEVELS
Melting glaciers at the poles will lead to rising sea levels, perhaps as much as a 3-ft. (1-m) sea level rise by 2100. That's a serious problem for low-lying places such as the Maldives. This group of islands is just over 3 ft. (1m) above sea level.

LOSS OF PROTECTIVE ICE
If the icecaps melt, it will speed up global warming. Snow and ice usually form a protective cooling layer over the polar regions. When that covering melts, Earth absorbs more sunlight and gets hotter.

The images below show how the amount of sea ice at the Arctic during the summer is decreasing.

SUMMER 1979–1981

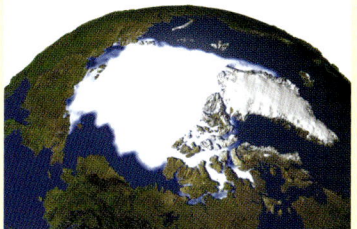

SUMMER 2003–2005

EXTINCTION
Polar bears hunt seals on the Arctic sea ice. If the icecap disappears, polar bears will lose their hunting ground and become extinct.

WONDERFUL WORLD

TAKING IT EASY WITH ENERGY

PLANNING FOR THE FUTURE
Some energy-saving solutions, like putting solar panels on a house, are more expensive at the start. But in the long run they reduce our need for fossil fuels to provide homes and businesses with heat and other energy.

EVERY LITTLE BIT COUNTS
Your local electricity and water companies offer many good ideas for conserving energy. Your family can install low-flow showerheads and toilets. You can turn down the heat in the winter—and wear a sweater!

CHAPTER 17:
Making a Difference

One way we can all help stop global warming is to use less energy. Using less energy and caring for Earth's natural resources will also help ensure that future generations have what they need to survive on our planet.

CUTTING GREENHOUSE GASES

Using less electricity means power plants will burn less fuel, such as coal and oil, which give off greenhouse gases. One of the most important ways that we can cut down greenhouse gases and reduce our use of natural resources is to use less oil. Walking or bicycling instead of using a car can make a big difference.

The more we know about our interaction with Earth and its natural resources, the better off we will be.

MAKING A DIFFERENCE

Many cities are looking into providing "clean" public transportation. In the future you might ride on buses and trains driven by solar power or other renewable forms of energy.

REUSE

In addition to reducing our need for resources, reusing and recycling are two ways we can all play a role in conserving energy. Reusing allows us to make a second (or third or fourth) use of an existing object. Plastic shopping bags and cardboard boxes can be used over and over again. If we reuse things, less energy is needed to make new items.

Often, reducing energy consumption can also improve your health. Riding a bike or walking instead of driving can benefit both the planet and you.

This paper has been collected from recycling points and is waiting to be processed and recycled.

RECYCLE

Recycling allows us to make new things out of used materials. Many materials can be recycled such as paper, plastic, metal, and glass. Most communities have recycling programs that allow us all to easily dispose of metal cans, drink bottles, and paper. It takes less energy to make cans and bottles from old recycled metal than it does to make new bottles and cans.

WATER USE IN THE HOME

Here are some common uses of water in the home. Also shown is the average amount of water each activity uses.

- One bath: 21 gal. (80L)
- One shower: 9 gal. (35L)
- One toilet flush: 2 gal. (8L)
- One dishwasher load: 7 gal. (25L)
- One washing-machine load: 17 gal. (65L)

In an average home, which activity do you think uses the most water per day?

Answer: flushing the toilet

WATER-SAVING TIPS

SAVE AS YOU FLUSH
Most households use more water flushing the toilet than anything else. Your family can install a water-saving device in the toilet tank.

BE FULLY LOADED
Make sure you organize your laundry so that you don't need to wash items individually. Use the washing machine and dishwasher only when there's a full load.

CARING FOR EARTH'S WATER

Water is an important natural resource. It is essential to the survival of all life on Earth. However, it is so much a part of our everyday lives that it is easy to take it for granted.

WASTING WATER

Do you have any faucets that drip at home? One drip per second means that 1 gal. (4L) of water each day is escaping from your faucets. Do you leave the water running while you brush your teeth? Running the tap for only one minute can use around 3 gal. (10L) of water. An average adult in the U.S. uses between 130–160 gal. (500–600L) of water per day. It pours from our faucets—clean, safe, and ready to use.

We can ALL save water in our everyday lives.

Using a hose to wash a car makes the job easier. But rinsing with a hose can use the same amount of water as more than 30 buckets! Instead, wash a car using buckets of water. You will use a lot less.

MAKING A DIFFERENCE

Many children in the Third World have to walk three to four hours daily to fetch water.

Remember: only one percent of the water on Earth is usable fresh water. If we use the Earth's fresh water faster than nature can recycle it, there will not be enough fresh water to go around in the future.

WATER FOR ALL

Many people in less-developed countries around the world use only around 24 gal. (90L) of water per day. That water might be in a well far from their homes. And, what's more, the water could be dirty or diseased.

Around 1.2 billion people in the world today do not have access to clean water.

WATER-SAVING TIPS

WATER-SAVING YARDS

In half an hour, a lawn sprinkler can use as much water as a family of four uses in one day. Many people are now putting down stone or wood surfaces in their yards. They don't need a lot of water to look good. And they don't need to be mowed!

REUSING WATER

After you boil eggs or vegetables, save the water. When it has cooled down, you can use it to water the plants in your garden or yard. It will be full of nutrients, which will help the plants grow. You can also use the dirty water from fish tanks.

CLEAN WATER FOR ALL

Everyone on Earth should be able to use clean water every day.

Many organizations around the world are helping communities that do not have clean water. They raise funds to pay for wells to be dug and for water pumps and sanitation equipment to be installed.

You can help raise money for this work. You will find information about organizations involved on these websites:

www.charitywater.org

www.justadrop.org

www.unicef.org/wes

www.wateraid.org

GLOSSARY

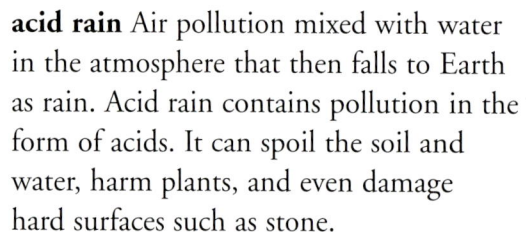

acid rain Air pollution mixed with water in the atmosphere that then falls to Earth as rain. Acid rain contains pollution in the form of acids. It can spoil the soil and water, harm plants, and even damage hard surfaces such as stone.

air pressure A force created by the weight of air pressing down on Earth's surface.

asthenosphere The thin pliable layer of Earth's upper mantle on which the rigid crust can move.

atmosphere The thick layer of air that surrounds Earth. The gases that make up Earth's atmosphere include nitrogen (78%) and oxygen (21%). There is also water and small quantities of other gases such as argon and carbon dioxide.

bacterium A type of single-celled organism that can be seen only under a microscope. Some bacteria cause diseases.

carbon dioxide (CO_2) A colorless, odorless gas that is present in Earth's atmosphere. It is produced naturally when humans and animals breathe out. It is also produced by burning fossil fuels such as coal and oil.

carbon monoxide A poisonous gas formed in the burning of fossil fuels.

convection A way that heat moves from one area to another. During convection, cool air sinks and warm air rises. This creates currents in the air that we feel as wind. Convection causes clouds, rain, and thunderstorms.

crust The outer layer of Earth. The crust is around 25 mi. (40km) thick beneath the continental landmasses and 4 mi. (7km) thick beneath the oceans.

decompose To decay or rot.

environment The objects and conditions, such as climate, soil, and living things, that surround and act upon a habitat. These things also affect the ecosystems that are part of that habitat.

extinct When an animal or plant no longer exists on Earth.

famine A severe shortage of food that can lead to starvation and disease.

fossil The remains of a once-living thing, such as an animal or a plant, preserved in rock.

glacier A huge slow-moving river of ice (around 100 ft./30m thick). A glacier moves slowly down a slope or valley.

global warming The gradual warming of Earth's atmosphere. Most scientists believe that this is caused by humans burning fossils fuels such as oil and coal. The burning of these fuels gives off greenhouse gases that trap too much of the Sun's heat in Earth's atmosphere.

gravity A natural force that pulls objects together. The bigger an object, the more gravitational force it has. Earth's gravity causes objects to fall toward it.

icecaps Huge permanently frozen areas of ice at the North and South poles.

igneous rocks Rocks formed from magma that has reached Earth's surface and cooled. To remember that igneous rocks are formed by great heat and fire, think of the word *ignite*.

irrigation The process of bringing water to a place. For example, pumping water from a river to irrigate (water) crops.

landfill A huge hole in the ground where many tons of garbage are buried. Eventually the garbage is covered over with soil.

lava Molten material made of rock, gas, and other debris that comes from an erupting volcano. Before it reaches the surface, this material is known as magma.

lithosphere The hard outer layer of Earth formed from the crust and the uppermost part of the mantle. On average, the lithosphere is around 60 mi. (100km) deep. The word *lithosphere* comes from the Greek word *lithos*, which means "stone."

magma The fiery, flowing mix of rock found in Earth's mantle and outer core. The heat and pressure inside Earth keeps the material in this semifluid state. When magma manages to escape to the surface of the planet, it is called lava.

minerals Solid inorganic substances that occur naturally on Earth such as copper, iron, and salt. Some minerals are used by plants and animals.

monsoon A seasonal wind that blows in different directions at different times of the year. In Asia, monsoon winds usually bring very heavy rains, often causing flooding.

nutrients The minerals and substances that plants and animals need to grow and develop.

organism A living thing.

particulates Small pieces of substances such as dirt, aerosol droplets, and other pollutants.

photosynthesis The way in which plants convert carbon dioxide and water into food (carbohydrates) by using the energy in sunlight.

politics A system of policies and practices influencing the actions of a group of people.

prey An animal that is hunted and eaten for food by another animal.

reservoir A place where liquids collect and are stored. Molten magma collects in natural reservoirs underground. People build reservoirs, such as lakes, to collect fresh water.

satellite A body that revolves around another larger body in space. The Moon is Earth's only natural satellite.

saturated Holding as much water or moisture as can be absorbed.

scavenger An animal that feeds on the bodies of animals that are already dead.

sediment Tiny grains of material such as rock and sand.

sleet A cold, slushy substance halfway between rain and snow. Sleet is caused by snowflakes melting as they fall to Earth because the ground temperature is above freezing.

smog A foglike haze caused by pollution in the air. The word is formed by combining the words *smoke* and *fog*.

solar system A group of planets orbiting a star such as the Sun.

static electricity A buildup of electricity in an object. It is often caused by friction. Static electricity can form inside a storm cloud. When it leaps to the ground, we see it as a lightning bolt.

temperate A climate that is mild—not too hot or too cold.

tidal power Energy harnessed from the natural movement of bodies of water such as oceans and lakes. Tidal power gets its energy from the natural rise and fall of the water at different times of the day.

tsunami A Japanese word for the huge and damaging waves caused by earthquake vibrations under the ocean.

whirlwind A whirling column of wind that is most likely to occur on hot, dry days. Whirlwinds are also called dust devils, due to the dust and dirt that they pick up.

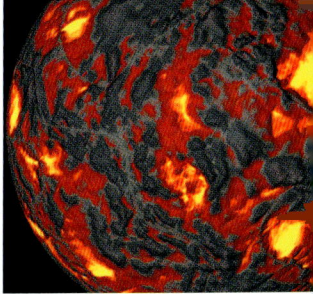

INDEX

A
abiotic factors 68–69, 70
acid rain 46, 90
asthenosphere 14, 15
atmosphere 7, 8, 9, 10, 11, 32, 40, 41, 42, 43, 44, 62, 63, 64, 65, 68, 69, 90, 95, 98

B
biomes 34, 57, 72–77
biotic factors 68

C
carbon cycle 63
carbon dioxide 8, 60, 63, 69, 95, 98, 105
climate 19, 32, 34–35, 57, 73, 76, 104–105
clouds 6–7, 36, 39, 41, 44–45, 46, 47, 48, 50, 51
continental drift 18–19
core 10, 11, 15, 16–17, 22
crust 8–9, 10, 11, 12–13, 14, 15, 20, 22, 23, 24, 25, 26, 27, 86, 87, 89, 92

D
deserts 34, 35, 50, 52, 56, 57, 68, 73, 76–77, 96, 105
droughts 33, 46, 53, 58, 76

E
earthquakes 8, 22, 24
ecosystems 54–71, 75, 76, 91, 94, 95, 98, 100–101
energy 24, 35, 36, 40, 58, 60, 61, 62, 66, 68, 71, 74, 75, 80, 82, 88, 90, 94, 95, 97, 98, 105, 106, 107
environment 14, 60, 64, 68, 70, 71, 100
erosion 28, 43
equator 10, 11, 34, 35, 36, 37, 43, 73
extinction 8, 83, 101, 105

F
faults 20, 21, 24
floods 33, 37, 46, 50, 52, 105
food chains 61, 66
forests 35, 45, 59, 71, 73, 85, 95, 99, 100
fossil fuels 86–87, 88–89, 90–91, 105, 106

G
geothermal power 96, 97
glaciers 19, 80, 105
global warming 38, 90, 104–105
gravity 39, 41, 93
greenhouse gases 104, 105, 106

H
habitats 57, 71, 95
hurricanes 32, 33, 50, 51, 52
hydroelectric power 96, 97

I
icecaps 35, 105
igneous rocks 27, 28
inorganic resources 28, 84

L
lava 11, 16, 22, 23, 25, 27, 28
lithosphere 20

M
magma 10, 11, 14, 22, 23, 27, 28
mantle 10, 11, 14–15, 20, 22, 25, 28
metamorphic rocks 27, 28
minerals 28, 29, 64–65, 67, 76, 80, 81, 83, 84, 92–93
monsoons 35, 37, 46, 52
Moon 6, 7, 47
mountains 6, 12, 13, 22, 25, 26, 39, 40, 57, 73, 76, 80

N
nitrogen 8, 41, 62, 64, 90
nonrenewable resources 82, 83, 86–93, 94
nutrients 62, 63, 69, 75, 95, 109

O
organic resources 84, 85
organisms 56, 61, 62, 84, 86, 95
oxygen 7, 14, 15, 40, 41, 60, 65, 69, 98

P
Pangaea 18–19
photosynthesis 60, 63, 68, 98
pollution 44, 90, 91

R
rain 11, 28, 32, 34, 35, 36, 37, 38, 39, 43, 44, 46–47, 48, 50, 52, 53, 58, 73, 76, 90
rainforests 35, 45, 68, 71, 72, 73, 98, 99, 101
renewable resources 80, 82, 83, 85, 94–101, 107
rocks 6, 7, 8, 11, 14, 15, 20, 24, 25, 26–27, 28, 43, 65, 68, 76, 84, 92, 93

S
sedimentary rocks 27, 28
snow 28, 32, 33, 35, 36, 38, 39, 43, 48–49, 50, 77, 105
soil 6, 11, 26, 34, 53, 56, 57, 60, 63, 64, 65, 67, 68, 69, 73, 76, 81, 83, 91, 95
solar
 power 96, 97, 107
 system 6, 7, 8, 9, 50
Sun 6, 7, 8, 9, 10, 16, 17, 32, 35, 36, 37, 38, 39, 40, 41, 42, 44, 46, 47, 58, 60, 61, 66, 68, 73, 74, 75, 77, 80, 94, 97, 105

T
tectonic plates 20, 22, 25
thunderstorms 32, 45, 46
tornadoes 50, 51
tsunamis 8, 24

V
volcanoes 11, 22–23, 27, 28, 38, 52, 65

W
water 6, 7, 8, 10, 11, 12, 13, 14, 23, 24, 26, 28, 32, 33, 34, 35, 36, 38–39, 44, 46, 49, 50, 52, 53, 56–57, 58, 60, 61, 62, 65, 68, 73, 74, 75, 76, 77, 80, 82, 83, 86, 87, 93, 94, 95, 97, 98, 105, 106, 108, 109
water cycle 38–39, 62, 68, 80
whirlwinds 50
wind 11, 17, 28, 32, 35, 42–43, 51, 52, 76, 80, 82, 94, 96, 105